GRAND CENTRAL TERMINAL

City within the City

Deborah Nevins,
General Editor

With a Foreword by
Jacqueline Kennedy Onassis

Essays by:
Deborah Nevins
Elliot Willensky
Elaine Abelson
Milton R. Newman
David Bonderman
Hugh Hardy

Book design: Keith Godard of Works

The Municipal
Art Society
of New York

This book was made possible with
generous funding from the
National Endowment for the Humanities.

■ With the U.S. Supreme Court's 1978 decision in the Grand Central Terminal case, landmark preservation law came of age.

□ Prior to this decision, lower courts had upheld those preservation regulations that applied to properties within designated historic districts. But the principal rationale underlying these decisions – that the burden of regulation on an individual landowner was offset by the advantage he derived from the shared benefits of the historic district – did not appear to support landmark regulation of individual buildings outside of historic districts. As a result, most local governments did not legislate mandatory restraints on individual landmarks, and in the few cities which had such restraints, enforcement was tentative and timid, particularly with respect to commercial properties in downtown areas with high real estate values.

□ In the Grand Central Terminal case, the City of New York, acting through its Landmarks Preservation Commission, applied its landmarks law to bar construction of a high-rise office tower which would have destroyed the aesthetic integrity of the terminal, a designated landmark in the heart of the city's central business district. The Supreme Court upheld this action despite the claim by the Penn Central Transportation Company, the owner of the terminal, that the railroad would receive several million dollars a year of additional revenues if the office tower were built. The Court stated, in effect, that the owner of a landmark cannot avoid regulation aimed at preserving the landmark simply by showing that a lot more money could be made by tearing it down or mutilating it to make way for another building.

□ The Court's decision makes it clear that landmark regulation has its limits: The owner cannot be required to maintain the landmark if the building, despite reasonably prudent management, is not economically viable. The regulatory scheme must provide – as does the New York City Landmarks Preservation Law – that the owner can be relieved of regulatory restraints upon an adequate showing of hardship. The criteria for determining hardship, both as a matter of constitutional law and of statutory interpretation of existing landmarks laws, are evolving and are very much in issue in such current controversies as the proposed office tower development on the Park Avenue site of Saint Bartholomew's Church. The law that will emerge will derive from the fundamental premises of the Grand Central Terminal decision: that is, that

landmarks regulation of both individual buildings and historic districts, undertaken purely to preserve our architectural and historical heritage, is constitutionally appropriate, and that such regulation cannot be challenged on the grounds that it prevents the "highest and best use" of the property – exploitation of its full development potential.

□ Following the Grand Central Terminal decision, dozens of American cities and towns have enacted landmarks preservation laws for the first time, or have amended preexisting laws to make them more effective. In those cities, such as New York, which already had effective landmark preservation laws in place, there has been a notable increase in the vigor and firmness with which the regulations are enforced.

□ Although the legal implications of the Grand Central Terminal decision are important indeed, its most powerful effect may well be symbolic. To the millions of Americans who have come to realize how vital, yet how fragile our architectural heritage is, the decision means that the fight can be won – even against the most powerful of corporations. The energy and determination derived from that understanding have imparted a new quality of maturity and enduring strength to the preservation movement.

Ralph C. Menapace
President
The Municipal Art Society of New York

1. Introduction and "Grand Central: Architecture as a Celebration of Daily Life," copyright © 1982 by Deborah Nevins.
2. "Grand Central: Shaper of a City," copyright © 1982 by Elliot Willensky.
3. "The Vanderbilt Connection," copyright © 1982 by Elaine Abelson.
4. "Grand Central: An Urban Toolbox," copyright © 1982 by Milton Newman.
5. "The Grand Central Terminal Litigation and the Development of Preservation Law," copyright © 1982 by David Bonderman.
6. "Saving Grand Central—Again," copyright © 1982 by Hugh Hardy.
7. Jacket design and art work/layout copyright © 1982 by Keith Godard.

ISBN: 0-9606892-2-2.
Library of Congress Catalog Number: 82-81177.
Printed in the United States of America.

CONTENTS

The Grand Central Terminal Exhibition appeals to Philip Morris for geographic and aesthetic reasons. The New York Central's graceful monument to railroading evokes a feeling of permanence. Its presence has become, quite literally, the foundation of a renaissance in the midtown area it dominates.
□ Our new Corporate World Headquarters building stands directly across from Grand Central on 42nd Street, its architecture reflecting and complementing the exquisite Beaux-Arts charm of one of New York's most important landmarks.
□ Our decision to stay in the heart of New York underscores Philip Morris's concern for the vitality of the central cities. In Richmond, Louisville, Milwaukee, St. Louis, New York, and elsewhere around the world, we have chosen to build or renovate within the city limits. In this, we are governed by our approach that our business activities must make social sense and our social activities must make business sense.
□ We can think of no finer way to celebrate our new home address than to support this salute to the imposing presence and vital influence of Grand Central.

George Weissman
Chairman of the Board and Chief Executive Officer
Philip Morris Incorporated

This book is published in conjunction with an exhibition of the same title that opened at the New-York Historical Society in May 1982. The exhibit received significant funding from Philip Morris Incorporated, whose statement on sponsorship appears above.

ACKNOWLEDGMENTS		6
FOREWORD	Jacqueline Kennedy Onassis	8
INTRODUCTION	Deborah Nevins	10
GRAND CENTRAL: ARCHITECTURE AS A CELEBRATION OF DAILY LIFE	Deborah Nevins	11
GRAND CENTRAL: SHAPER OF A CITY	Elliot Willensky	85
THE VANDERBILT CONNECTION	Elaine Abelson	109
GRAND CENTRAL: AN URBAN TOOLBOX	Milton R. Newman	121
THE GRAND CENTRAL TERMINAL LITIGATION AND THE DEVELOPMENT OF PRESERVATION LAW	David Bonderman	129
SAVING GRAND CENTRAL — AGAIN	Hugh Hardy	135
THE DESIGNERS OF GRAND CENTRAL		142
SOME FACTS ABOUT GRAND CENTRAL		143
BIOGRAPHIES OF THE AUTHORS		145
PICTURE CREDITS		145
THE MODEL		147

■ This book is dedicated to the Law Department of the City of New York, in particular Leonard J. Koerner and Nina Gershon, and to Dorothy Miner, Counsel for the Landmarks Preservation Commission of the City of New York; their valiant efforts in the preparation and arguing of the appeals in the now legendary Grand Central Terminal case before the U.S. Supreme Court have secured an architectural heritage for future generations of Americans.

■ In the years since this exhibition was conceived in the storefront office of the Committee to Save Grand Central, it has been nurtured by the skills, judgment, and kindness of hundreds of people. The Municipal Art Society is grateful for the help of all those who have brought this show and book into being, and wishes to express its appreciation for the special contributions of the following individuals and organizations.

□ We thank the National Endowment for the Humanities for its generous financial support of the project, enabling us to bring the story of Grand Central to a national audience.

□ We wish to thank Philip Morris Incorporated for its financial support, and the staff of its Office for Cultural Affairs – particularly Stephanie French and Marilynn Donini – for their generous and spirited participation in the completion of the exhibition plans.

□ We are also grateful for the additional support of the National Endowment for the Arts, and to Avery Brooke, whose love for Grand Central helped inspire us to do this project.

□ To our Board of Directors we owe special thanks, particularly to: Ralph Menapace, President of the Society, and Paul Byard, its Counsel, whose firsthand knowledge of the Grand Central litigation made them invaluable advisers to the exhibition planners; Ronald Freelander, whose enthusiasm revived this project more than once; Hugh Hardy, whose proverbial fascination with old railroad stations inspired and sustained this exhibition; Jacqueline Onassis, whose tireless efforts on behalf of the terminal have, deservedly, made her part of its legend; and Frederic Papert, whose leadership in the fight to save Grand Central made him a gallant champion of this exhibition.

□ To Senators Daniel Patrick Moynihan and Jacob K. Javits, Mayor Edward I. Koch, and Landmarks Preservation Commissioner Kent L. Barwick, for their stalwart advocacy and defense of the terminal, we wish to express our thanks and appreciation.

□ We are also grateful for the guidance of our board's Exhibit Committee and its staff: Mary Black, for her expert suggestions during the final planning stages; Alan Freedman, without whose sagacity and personal commitment this exhibition would not exist; Brendan Gill, for his continuing devotion to the cause of Grand Central; Elliot Willensky, whose polymathic command of the urban arts informs every aspect of the show and this book; Trudy Kramer, whose perspicacious questions moved us from proposal to story boards to packing cases; Norman Pfeiffer, of Hardy Holzman Pfeiffer, whose vision and practicality have been assets from the beginning; and Margot Wellington, Executive Director of the Society, whose resourcefulness in providing the materials and talent for the project's many details deserves commendation. Laurie Beckelman, former Deputy Director of the Society, organized the administration of the exhibition during its crucial first phases; it is hard to imagine the show without her. There are hardly words to express our gratitude to Henry Ng, Deputy Director of the Society, whose exceptional administrative abilities, good humor, and insight made this project possible.

□ For their invaluable and painstaking assistance in completing this book and mounting the exhibition, we owe special thanks to a number of individuals. Deborah Nevins served as exhibition curator and general editor of this book. Her knowledge and perception came to bear on every phase of the project, from the initial grant proposal through the finishing touches. Keith Godard, of Works, who designed this book and the exhibition poster and brochure, and editor Sara Blackburn not only performed their responsibilities on the most professional level, but did so with great creativity. Publication coordinator Charlie Roberts was a constant support. The firm of Hardy Holzman Pfeiffer Associates designed the exhibition with great imagination and consistently located the visual appeal of historical details.

□ We wish to thank Elaine Abelson, David Bonderman, Hugh Hardy, Deborah Nevins, Milton Newman, and Elliot Willensky, whose essays will contribute to architectural and preservation history long after the exhibition closes and whose work provided important background for the show's planners.

□ For the scholarly advice, technical expertise, and helpful criticism that they so selflessly shared, we are grateful to Tom Bender; Deborah Dinowitz and Sarah Sill, our attorneys at Cahill, Gordon & Reindel; Hugh Dunne; Leda Goldsmith; Robert Gutman; Carol Herselle Krinsky; Dorothy Miner; Gene Secunda and our friends at J. Walter Thompson; Bayrd Still; and William H. Whyte, Jr.

□ The assistance and resourcefulness of the staffs of many libraries and museums were essential for preparing the exhibition and book. Of particular help were: Wendy Shadwell, Helena Zinkham, Catherine Richards, and Wayne Goldstein at the New-York Historical Society; Janet Parks and Charling Fagan of Avery Library at Columbia University; and Nancy Kessler-Post, Steve Miller, and J. P. Hayden of the Museum of the City of New York.

□ We would like to acknowledge the various contributions of Vivian Awner, Susan Hillberg, Mary Alice Kennedy, Lex Lalli, Lexann Roland, Richard Rudich, Rebecca Shanor, and Meg Shore. For fine work under pressure, we are grateful to copy editor Marcia Lawther and proofreader Anne Phalon. Carole Sorell Inc. carried out the publicity for the exhibition with marvelous sensitivity to its content. Julius Potocsny and Nelson Breen brought their considerable skills to bear on the production of the film, sponsored by Philip Morris, that accompanies the exhibition. We wish to thank Stephen Saitas of Hardy Holzman Pfeiffer and Jeri Froehlich of Works for their unstinting dedication to the design of the exhibition and book. Victor Gong's early contributions as a member of Hardy Holzman Pfeiffer's design team were invaluable.

□ Finally, to those thousands of people who rallied to the defense of Grand Central, we offer our thanks and our exhibition.

■ Let us now praise Grand Central Station.

□ The battle to save it marked a turning point in how Americans value their architectural heritage. When the Committee to Save Grand Central Station was formed in 1975 it was joined by supporters from all over the country. As the case was argued and appealed to the United States Supreme Court it became apparent that it was not just a New York issue. When the Supreme Court ruled in its favor it saved for us, in its original state, the majestic building which has a place in so many people's memories, so many people's lives.

□ Progress had been made since that dismal time in 1963 when Philip Johnson, Aline Saarinen, Peter Blake, Norval White, Eliza Parkinson, Ulrich Franzen, and Peter Samton picketed alone in the snow to save Pennsylvania Station. That battle was lost, and the loss is irreparable.

□ Great civilizations of the past recognized that their citizens had aesthetic needs, that great architecture gave nobility and respite to their daily lives. They built fine buildings, spacious parks, beautiful markets. Their places of assembly, of worship, of ceremony, of arrival and departure were not merely functional but spoke to the dignity of man.

□ A young country, constantly re-forming its image of itself, the United States tore down too much. We saw great buildings and cherished small-scale neighborhoods disappear. The voice of preservationists was a lonely voice, powerless against mighty commercial interests.

□ But then the tide turned, the Landmarks Preservation Commission was formed and Americans began to realize that it would never be possible to build in the future as they had in the past, that old buildings are a precious part of our heritage, and that we cripple ourselves if we destroy them.

□ New York City is the center of civilization in our day as Athens, Rome, Persepolis were in theirs. Her citizens have recognized that by banding together they can save its loved buildings from destruction. From a young couple painstakingly renovating a brownstone, to artists fighting to keep old warehouses as studios, to workmen redoing the cast iron bridges in Central Park, to the Municipal Art Society saving the Villard Houses and installing in them the situation room of urban planning, we see the preservation effort here gather momentum as it has throughout the country.

□ This exhibition honors Grand Central Terminal. As a railroad station it works superbly. The originality and durability of its design solutions still leave transportation planners awestruck. As architecture it continues to give solace. Let us salute it for what it has meant in the past and for what it has done for the future.

■ One of the first buildings the New York City Landmarks Preservation Commission designated after its formation in 1965 was, in 1967, Grand Central Terminal. Just one year later, in 1968, the Penn Central Transportation Company, the owners of Grand Central Terminal, decided to build a fifty-five-story skyscraper over the terminal. In effect, this would have destroyed the landmark qualities of the building. The City of New York took Penn Central to court, and there followed a series of judicial decisions in New York State which eventually upheld the city's position. In 1978, the United States Supreme Court confirmed the validity of the landmark status of Grand Central Terminal.

□ The Committee to Save Grand Central Station, formed in 1975 by The Municipal Art Society, worked passionately to keep the issue alive and the public informed during the difficult years of court struggle. Through press conferences, advertising, rallies, and the organization of a special train ride from New York to Washington, D.C., the committee raised the consciousness of the public not only about the necessity of saving the terminal, but about the crucial importance of preserving the nation's cultural heritage. After the 1978 Supreme Court decision, The Municipal Art Society decided to sponsor an exhibition on Grand Central Terminal. But why sponsor an exhibition and book *after* the fight has been won?

□ The answer is that the terminal is still not safe from destruction. We must understand that misuse and brutal alteration can destroy it in a manner almost as complete as any planned physical demolition. The kinds of stores and services provided in the terminal must be attuned to the city's needs and attract users; urban mass transit must develop better connections to the railroad to make the building a viable transportation center. Storefronts, signage, and construction in the terminal must respect its enduring aesthetic qualities. The darkest specter of all may be the legal one. Changes in judicial philosophy could conceivably once again open the question of landmark status.

□ This book and the exhibition of the same title, *Grand Central Terminal: City Within the City*, are directed primarily to a general audience, although there is much that will be new to those who already know a great deal about New York City. Our project is, of course, intended to convey why Grand Central should be a landmark, but it has a more far-reaching goal: We hope it is a vehicle to dramatize the workings of architecture – the influences that come to bear on a building's form, and how the building affects the environment around it. In a sense we are presenting an intimate biography of a building, its ancestry, the forces which shaped its physical form and character, its interaction with the world, its life today, and its legacy to the future.

□ The origins of Grand Central in nineteenth-century New York, the reasons behind the decision to build it on 42nd Street, and the enormous consequences of this decision for the twentieth-century form of the city are skillfully woven together here by Elliot Willensky. The personality of the Vanderbilt family and their mighty influence on American railroading are also part of the heritage of Grand Central, as Elaine Abelson's lively essay elaborates. The process by which the design of Grand Central evolved, and the relation of the building to the world of architecture at the turn of the century, are analyzed by Deborah Nevins. Milton Newman brings his wit and perception to bear on why Grand Central is a paradigm of good urban design. Attorney David Bonderman explains the laws of survival for Grand Central in the context of the history of preservation law. Hugh Hardy is the internist, who presents the prognosis for Grand Central's future and suggests the medicine for the terminal's healthy survival. The essential lesson of Grand Central is that building site, function, and city can be magnificently integrated in a dynamic way to enhance the lives of all those who dwell in cities.

Deborah Nevins

Deborah Nevins

A Glory of the Metropolis

Railway stations possess for a city something of the importance that is possessed for a country by railways themselves. It is by no means an idle or empty boast, therefore, for New York to proclaim that from to-day it will have in use for itself and its daily army of visitors what are beyond question two railway stations [Grand Central Terminal and Pennsylvania Station] in every way superior to any other buildings for their purpose in the world.

□ This is a fact creditable alike to the metropolis, which has justified the erection here of structures so enormously expensive, and to the corporations, which have expended their millions in no mean and narrow spirit of hard utilitarianism, but with appreciation of a civic duty to produce architectural monuments of a kind calculated to illustrate and to educate the aesthetic taste of a great Nation. The New York Times, February 2, 1913

■ From the day of its opening in 1913, Grand Central, built by the New York Central Railroad and designed by the architectural firms of Warren and Wetmore and Reed and Stem, has been hailed as the largest and the greatest railroad terminal in the world. It has become one of the most resonant symbols of New York and a metaphor for intensity, bustle, and vitality – "just like Grand Central Station," the saying goes. The building is a benchmark in the history of architecture; no other railroad station would be built to rival it in any way before the end of the railroad era and the beginning of the airplane and automobile age.

□ Grand Central Terminal is, however, more than an elegant Beaux-Arts building with a huge interior concourse. It is part of a great urban mixed-use complex of connected hotels and office buildings. Today the terminal itself houses offices, stores of all kinds, restaurants, police offices, and even a tennis club; at one time it contained both an art gallery and a movie theater. The terminal was, moreover, an engineering marvel of its time. Its double level "bunk bed" track plan, carrying electrically operated trains, is still admired for the inventiveness of its conception. The advent of electrified trackage meant that the open or only partially closed tunnels previously necessary for steam engines could now be closed, allowing the development of the land on either side of Park Avenue. Because the tunnels could now be paved over, the railroad devised the novel idea of constructing buildings over the tracks to produce new revenue for the company. It was in this way that the character of the street changed from one of industrial buildings, lower-class homes, and small wooden structures to an elegant thoroughfare with all the connotations of wealth and charm worthy of the name Park Avenue.[1]

□ But the importance of the terminal goes beyond what the eye can see. In order to understand its conceptual richness as a still-functioning symbol of the turn-of-the-century period in which it was conceived, we might think of the terminal as a panoramic display of the scientific and cultural wares of its time. This remarkable building synthesizes all of those nineteenth-century developments that allowed for the conception of the terminal's twentieth-century scale and complexity. Steel construction and electricity were the underpinnings of the building's physical form. But it was the invention of multitiered administrative hierarchies developed by the first corporations – the railroads – that harnessed investment, manpower, and new technology into a functioning unit. Without this administrative capability, the terminal's scale, and the urbanistic vision that accompanied it, would have been impossible.

□ In January 1903 the New York Central decided that it would hold a limited architectural competition for the design of a new railroad terminal on 42nd Street, and, further, that it would expand the system's trackage, electrify all trains entering the terminal, and develop the area north of the terminal by leasing air rights over the tracks to developers – even though in 1898 and again in 1900, the company had gone to great expense and some considerable inconvenience to remodel the original Grand Central Depot of 1869–1871. In 1898 a new facade had been constructed around that station and three stories had been added. In 1900 the interior had been remodeled, combining separate waiting rooms into one, and expanding the trackage. What precipitated a decision that would cause the disruption of the railroad's normal terminal operations – although, amazingly, not of normal service – for many years? What moved the railroad to expend huge sums of money, and to extend its property so that it would eventually own an irregularly shaped strip of land from 42nd to 50th streets between Madison and Lexington avenues, with a tongue of land most of the width of Park Avenue from 51st Street to 59th Street? The decision was actually a gradual process, initiated when growing traffic congestion and public pressure to increase the system's safety resulted in the railroad's move to electrify.

11

□ Between 1890 and 1910 railroad passenger traffic doubled; the number of steam engines using the open-cut Park Avenue tunnel created an overheated, smoky environment that became intolerable for passengers and resulted in a series of accidents that were regarded with increasing anger on the part of the public. In 1901 the district attorney for New York called a grand jury to investigate charges of criminal negligence against the railroad. On January 8, 1902, fifteen people were killed in a collision in the Park Avenue tunnel, and by May 7, 1903, the New York State Legislature decreed that by July of 1908 no steam-run trains could enter the city south of the Harlem River. The railroad moved ahead with plans to fulfill the stipulation before it became law.

□ The credit for originating the plan to electrify, and for gradually developing the extraordinary scheme which laid the foundation for the station of today, belongs to William J. Wilgus, in 1899 the chief engineer of the railroad. Wilgus was a high school graduate whose creative genius was his ability to envision the urbanistic consequences of electrification.

□ In an 1899 conversation between William Wilgus and Frank J. Sprague, who is credited as the inventor of electric traction, Sprague suggested that the Yonkers branch of the New York Central's Putnam division be electrified.[2] Stimulated by their discussion, Wilgus himself devised a plan which contained the germ of some of the most ingenious aspects of the future terminal. He suggested that the suburban trains that fed into the terminal be electrified and placed on a lower level of tracks ending in a loop under the station. This plan was approved by the railroad in 1900. By 1901, pedestrian access to the new IRT subway and expanded trackage were added to the plan.

□ By the end of 1902 the Wilgus plan had evolved to the point where it called for the total electrification of all trains that entered the terminal; the enlargement of the railroad yard and trackage; and the replacement of the station itself by a sixteen- to twenty-story skyscraper that would contain a hotel, commercial offices, and possibly even a department store and a theater. Wilgus also added to the plan the unusual idea of an elevated drive which would allow traffic to continue uninterrupted along Park Avenue.

□ In early 1903, Wilgus made dramatic additions to his concept, which would have tremendous effect on the future of the city. He proposed that all terminal facilities below 56th Street be rebuilt and that air rights over the expanded trackage under Park Avenue be developed (with the establishment of a realty company to manage the resulting properties). This planned complex of mixed-use buildings over railroad land was eventually labeled Terminal City.[3] It was envisioned that the income from these properties would offset the enormous cost of electrification. (The estimate in 1902 was $10 million for electrification, and another $4 million for trackage, an amount which, translated into 1980 terms, would be the equivalent of $355 million.[4] The land and construction costs of the building were estimated in 1903 at $43 million; the final cost in 1913 was approximately $80 million.)[5] The Terminal City scheme was totally dependent on electric trackage and steel skyscraper construction. Steel construction obviated the need for a continuous foundation wall to support the building; instead, the building's load could be transferred to a series of steel columns which, in this case, would straddle the tracks.

□ The architects who were invited to submit designs for the limited competition of 1903 included the New York firm of McKim, Mead and White, who would complete their Pennsylvania Station in New York City in 1910, and the Chicago firm of D. H. Burnham and Company, who had been the chief planners of the 1893 Columbian Exposition in Chicago, and who would be the designers of Union Station (1903–1907) in Washington, D.C.,

Union Station, Washington, D.C.

as well as the Flatiron Building in New York City (1902). Both the McKim and Burnham firms were among the most successful in the country at the time.

□ The only two other entries were submitted by the firms of Samuel Huckel, Jr. of Philadelphia,

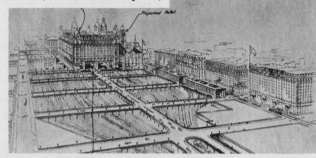

Competition entry by Samuel Huckel, Jr.

who had worked for Wilgus on the interior renovations of the station in 1900, and Reed and Stem, of St. Paul, who were already engaged in other work for the New York Central. Reed and Stem won the competition, but corporate and family connections would decree that their role was to be only as collaborators with the firm of Warren and Wetmore.

□ McKim, Mead and White's entry was distinctive for its sixty-story tower emerging from the fourteen-story terminal building below it.

Competition entry by McKim, Mead and White.

A 300-foot jet of steam spraying forth from the tower and illuminated at night by red lights would have made their terminal a landmark of extraordinary power, surely visible from the waterfront borders of Brooklyn and Queens. If executed, the structure would have been taller than the Woolworth Building (1911–1913) in lower Manhattan. At the turn of the century, in fact, it would have been the tallest building in the world.

□ McKim, Mead and White's design had solved the problem of urban circulation around the terminal by allowing Park Avenue and the cross streets to run straight through the building, a proposal especially sensitive to the movement of people and traffic. The submissions of D. H. Burnham and Company have been lost, but we can assume that they, like the others, used the standard classical vocabulary of the large civic buildings of the day; we are probably also safe in assuming that the firm conceived of the terminal as a tall building.

□ Charles Reed's sister had been married in 1892 to Wilgus, but it was surely not on this basis alone that his firm won the competition. In terms of urban planning, the firm's design was clearly an imaginative and highly resolved solution to the terminal's requirements. All three of the existing competition schemes connected the north and south sections of Park Avenue, contained some kind of office structure, and either attached a hotel to the terminal or planned for one between 43rd and 44th streets west of it. But Reed and Stem, in their response to Wilgus's requirement to connect both parts of Park Avenue,

Competition entry by Reed and Stem.

devised a wide elevated roadway around the terminal, a "circumferential plaza," as it was called. Instead of stairways within the terminal, they planned gently sloping ramps for the convenience of travelers. These two ideas are among the terminal's most sophisticated elements, devices which still aid the comfort of those on foot as well as those in cars.

□ Although it is unclear whether it was an original part of their entry or whether it was submitted soon after they won the competition, Reed and Stem devised a stunning plan for the development of the terminal's north end. They conceived of this area as a "court of honor."[6]

"Court of Honor" for Park Avenue north of the terminal, proposed by Reed and Stem.

The classical vocabulary and uniform scale of the buildings enclosing the court on two sides formed a closed vista from upper Park Avenue and presented a vision reminiscent of archaeological reconstructions of ancient Rome. It was suggested that the National Academy of Design and the Metropolitan Opera would take up residence in this complex, creating a center for the arts in conjunction with one of the greatest transportation centers in the world.

□ The Reed and Stem scheme was never realized, but it provided the basis for how the railroad would continue to plan for the future development of the area north of the terminal.

Park Avenue north of Grand Central before the development of the air rights sites.

Proposals for the development of Park Avenue (postcards).

A number of postcards, periodical illustrations, and advertisements published after 1910 depict the railroad's projected development of Terminal City as a series of buildings stretching north from the terminal, all with classical vocabulary and uniform cornice line. In spite of the fact that the structures that used the air rights eventually were designed by several different architectural firms – including a number by Warren and Wetmore – they nonetheless created a precinct of high-rise buildings in the city where a common aesthetic prevailed – the use of Classical and Renaissance sources as inspiration. In 1929, the New York Central Building (now the Helmsley Building) opened at 45th Street, and its broad arms and tower closed the vista from upper Park Avenue and created a monumental boundary to this unique architectural environment. The life of this enclave was brief, for it was soon to be replaced by the glass skyscrapers of the 1950s.

□ The architecture of the finished terminal, as well as the very notion of developing a great urban complex at a single stroke, were both stunning examples of the aftereffects of the 1893 Columbian Exposition in Chicago. This fair, which came to be known as the White City, had featured a coordinated complex of Renaissance and Baroque revival buildings.[7] The main buildings, of uniform sixty-foot cornice line, were arranged around a central court. The White City was an exceptionally important stimulus in the development of a planning philosophy known as the City Beautiful movement as well as of the American Renaissance style that accompanied it. The aesthetic preference of the City Beautiful movement was for the architectural vocabulary of Italian Renaissance and European Baroque architecture, and, in some instances, for Roman buildings. The city planners of the City Beautiful movement likewise looked for inspiration to the axial arrangement of streets and broad avenues of Italian Baroque city planning, and to the mid-nineteenth-century Baroque-style renovations of Paris by Baron Haussmann.

□ It was the financial power of corporations and philanthropists, as well as large municipalities, that supported the comprehensive planning schemes and the American Renaissance style which this movement engendered in America. The idea of city renewal flourished at the end of the period 1870–1910, an era which had witnessed tremendous growth in the size and population concentration of American cities. Accompanying this economic growth and the population shift from a rural to an urban America was the expansion of cultural institutions for the public benefit – art museums, libraries, museums of natural history, opera houses, large universities, as well as transportation networks, in particular, urban mass transit and railroads.

□ The models for the City Beautiful movement's architectural style were large public buildings of the past that seemed to fit both the physical requirements and the intellectual and emotional inclinations of philanthropists, governments, and cultural institutions, all building with wealth acquired in the post-Civil War era. In constructing these often-massive public buildings, the sponsors' social and economic power became symbolically linked to the great cultures of Rome and the Renaissance. Cities of clean streets, public parks, and improved transportation systems, beautified by public art and Renaissance Revival architecture, were widely regarded as morally and spiritually uplifting.

□ At the turn of the century, New York, like other major cities of the time, was engaged in debate about the formation of a comprehensive city plan.[8] Clearly, this debate affected those who would be responsible for the terminal. In 1898 Charles Harder called for a New York City plan of diagonal avenues with a practical, functional base that would coordinate New York's transportation facilities with its manufacturing areas. In the same vein, the MacMillan plan of 1901–1902 for Washington, D.C., called for that city's transformation into a graceful environment of broad vistas and diagonal streets.

□ Stimulated by Harder's ideas and by the Washington proposal, in 1902 the Fine Arts Federation, The Municipal Art Society, and *The New York Times* urged Mayor Seth Low to form a commission to evolve an official plan for New York. Low did not immediately sponsor a commission, but The Municipal Art Society convened a conference on November 29, 1902, just four days before the Grand Central Terminal competition was announced. The conference report called for improvement in transportation, the construction of civic centers and public monuments, and the extension of the park system. It took until 1904 to establish a commission under Mayor George McClellan, who succeeded Low, and its final report was not submitted until January 1907. Whitney Warren, who was to become the chief aesthetician of Grand Central, was a member of the commission. In principal the new report

called for many of the same improvements that the 1902 document had urged but developed the requirements in greater detail. (The report included a proposal to widen 42nd Street

Approach to Blackwell's Island Bridge. The McClellan Report of 1907.

and to relieve the congestion around Grand Central by submerging its east-west traffic in a tunnel that would bypass the intersection of Fifth Avenue!)

□ Concerned New Yorkers brought their involvement with City Beautiful ideas to the plans for the building of Grand Central. On March 13, 1903, *The New York Times* published a letter from the Fine Arts Federation, proposing that the terminal should be conceived in a scale and with the attention to aesthetics which fitted the federation's conception of it as a monument. (It appears that the public had little or no knowledge of the railroad's competition, which was ending in that month.) The federation urged that in undertaking the improvements on such a "commanding site," the railroad "not lose the great opportunity offered for developing these improvements on artistic lines so that the station may be a monument and an ornament to the city, with beautiful and dignified approaches such as we are in the habit of seeing in some of the European cities. . . ." The letter goes on to note that a railroad station "belongs to the public in a greater degree than the buildings which are constructed by the municipality, the state or the Federal government. . . ."[9] The organization also suggested that an architectural competition be held for the station, for which they would be happy to appoint a committee. Wilgus, the fifth vice-president of the railroad, replied that the New York Central had already acted along the lines the federation had suggested.

Grand Central Terminal 1903–1913

□ Reed and Stem's joy at winning the competition would be fleeting. Shortly after the competition was judged, Whitney Warren, with his partner, Charles Wetmore, presented their own design for the new terminal to the railroad's committee. Warren's friend and cousin, William K. Vanderbilt, chairman of the New York Central Corporation and the Commodore's grandson, seems to have brought his influence to bear on what followed. The result was that Whitney Warren and his partner formed an agreement of association on February 8, 1904 with Reed and Stem. Charles Reed was designated the executive head of the work; each firm maintained a separate office. The fee for the work, to be paid jointly to the associated architects and then to be divided by themselves, was set at the following percentages of the final cost of the completed building: 1 percent for preliminary plans, 2 percent for working drawings and specifications, and 1 percent for supervision of the work.[10] Approximately six years of continuous work on the design followed. The scheme, the basic outlines of which form the building of today, was completed by 1910, and construction began the same year.

□ We are exceptionally fortunate that we have a record of the Grand Central design process – the set of drawings by way of which the final design was achieved. This design saga starts with Warren and Wetmore presenting a scheme that differed completely from Reed and Stem's winning submission. The surviving Warren and Wetmore submission to the railroad, unpublished until now,[11] is presumably their original entry, as it has only their own firm's name on it. It is a lower building than the one conceived by Reed and Stem.

□ In the designs of 1905 and 1907

Warren and Wetmore scheme for Grand Central Terminal, dated 1903, redated 1904.

Warren and Wetmore scheme for Grand Central Terminal, dated 1903, redated 1904.

the elevation is closer to the terminal as completed in 1913, but in both designs the circumferential plaza has disappeared, as has the innovative Reed and Stem system of interior ramps. In the 1905 project, the large interior concourse is enclosed by intersecting vaults expressed on the exterior; in the 1907 version, the roof takes a lower profile, and now closely resembles what would be the final design. By 1909, the circumferential plaza and the interior ramp system had been restored to the design; the New Haven Railroad, which had the right of approval on the project as a lessee of the station, had unexpectedly insisted that the ramps be restored. By 1910,

Warren and Wetmore scheme for Grand Central Terminal, dated 1903, redated 1904.

Most commentators have observed that Warren and Wetmore summarily discarded Reed and Stem's ideas of a circumferential plaza and the ramp system, but this early design includes the elevated plaza. With the exception of this feature, there is little else that connects it to the winning competition scheme.

□ The Warren and Wetmore scheme of 1903–1904 has all the characteristics of a French Beaux-Arts facade, basically divided in three parts, with the middle story the tallest. (This arrangement is not unlike the submissions for the U.S. Customs House competition in New York in 1899, particularly those of H. J. Hardenberg and Carrère and Hastings.)[12] The building's section and its multilobed dome recall Parisian designs of the 1890s. The spectacular elevated plaza, ringed with sculpture, is also a cosmopolitan evocation of French aesthetics. Three arched openings of the lower section of the main facade are meshed with the "window wall" of the middle section to form what would become in the final design of today a wall of three arched windows.

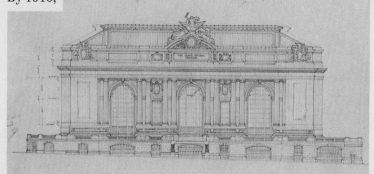

the clean, jewel-box outlines of the facade as we know it had been set, and early in the year construction began.

□ Neither Wilgus nor the firm of Reed and Stem would participate in the final design and construction of the terminal. Wilgus, in a disagreement with the railroad, resigned in 1907. His responsibilities were assumed by two men, George Kittredge and George Harwood. Soon the Reed and Stem firm's disassociation with the project would become an affair.

□ On November 12, 1911, Charles Reed died. On November 16, the day after the funeral, Wetmore, originally trained as a lawyer, wrote to the railroad suggesting that Warren and Wetmore have sole responsibility for the terminal from then on. In December a new agreement was drawn up without consulting Allen Stem. Stem eventually sued Warren and Wetmore for their share of the architectural fees, and the case was decided on July 17, 1916, in favor of Reed and Stem. Stem and the Reed estate were awarded $219,000, which included interest. The case was appealed in 1919, the earlier decision was upheld, and the case was appealed again in 1920. In this second and final appeal, Reed and Stem again prevailed, and were awarded $500,000. This included 2 percent of the building cost of the terminal and 1.5 percent of the cost of the Biltmore Hotel, for which they had done preliminary work. In that same year Whitney Warren was expelled from the American Institute of Architects, presumably as a result of his actions after Reed's death. Nonetheless, Warren and Wetmore maintained their very profitable New York practice.

□ In the end, the terminal turned out to be a synthesis of the thinking of three important factions: Wilgus, Reed and Stem, and Warren and Wetmore. Wilgus's double level trackage concept remained a constant element throughout the design process, and although the loop configuration of the tracks was removed at various stages, it was incorporated into the final scheme. Wilgus's air-rights development proposal was also a constant element. While Reed and Stem's contribution was the ramp system and the circumferential drive, Warren and Wetmore were responsible for the elevation and for the general *parti*, or character and form of the building, as well as for its imagery and finesse.

□ The outside dimensions of the building measure 301 feet by 722 feet 6 inches. There are forty-two tracks on the express level and twenty-five tracks on the suburban or lower level, with additional tracks for storage and service. The exterior of the building was constructed with Stony Creek, Connecticut granite and Bedford, Indiana limestone. The interior

was finished with walls of imitation Caen limestone and detailing of beige Bottocino marble, the floor of Tennessee marble.

□ The vaults on the terminal's lower level were constructed with tiles in the Guastavino technique – a lightweight, thin-shelled method that affords great flexibility in construction – which was also used in such important New York buildings as the Cathedral of St. John the Divine. Although the building gives the appearance of stone construction, the entire structure is supported by a variety of sophisticated steel construction techniques;

Grand Central Terminal under construction.

the large, impressive piers in the main concourse are only casings for the actual supports, made of steel.

□ Perhaps, it has been said, to recall the fact that travelers of the past had been guided by the stars, the vault of the main concourse of the building is painted to depict the constellations.

Interior of Grand Central (postcard).

The painting is from a design by the French artist Paul Helleu, who included tiny light bulbs of diverse intensity in the depiction, to portray the varying luminosity of the stars. The scheme shows the constellations reversed – that is, seen as if looking down from the heavens. It has been suggested both that the design was derived from a medieval manuscript which portrayed the sky in such a way and that it was an unconscious mistake on the part of Helleu or the painters.[13]

□ The sculpture of Mercury with Hercules and Minerva that tops the terminal's main facade, designed by Jules-Alexis Coutan, professor at the Ecole des Beaux-Arts in Paris,[14] was executed by Donnelly and Ricci and by William Bradley and Sons.

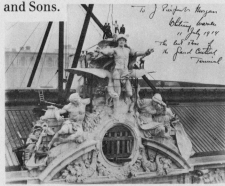

Carved in separate sections from Bedford limestone, the elements were secured together only when mounted on the building. According to Whitney Warren, the sculpture signified

. . . the glory of commerce, as typified by Mercury, supported by moral and mental energy – Hercules and Minerva. All to attest that this great enterprise has grown and exists not merely from the wealth expended, nor by the revenue derived, but by the brain and brawn constantly concentrated upon its development for nearly a century.[15]

The group measures sixty feet in width and fifty feet in height and weighs 1,500 tons. To complete this exterior symbolism, a statue of Commodore Vanderbilt was placed on the elevated drive below.

□ The synthesis of the design and engineering talents that made Grand Central gave us a complex, very American, Beaux-Arts building. Its extraordinary engineering and planning elements are cased in the vocabulary of the American Renaissance, here specifically in the canon of French eighteenth-century architecture. The American Renaissance mode was distinguished from most European Beaux-Arts structures of the turn of the century by its greater simplicity of ornamentation.

□ The formal, dignified, classical vocabulary of the Beaux-Arts architecture used in the terminal evokes the power of the corporation which built it. But the imagery of Grand Central goes beyond this particularly American level of symbolism. Employed here are the use of Roman models for its spatial organization – specifically, Roman bath architecture – as well as the generalized use of a Roman form for the facade – an arch of triumph.

□ Because railroad stations were widely regarded as the symbolic gateway to the city, the triumphal arch motif was particularly appropriate. American railroad stations from the late 1890s on typically featured an elevation which, in its succession of arches on the main facade, recalled this Roman form. This exterior imagery was first used in America for the facade of Charles Atwood's (a member of the firm of D. H. Burnham) temporary station at the 1893 exposition in Chicago, for which the interior space was inspired by the Roman baths. As the historian Carroll Meeks[16] has pointed out, Atwood's building was a stimulus for the elevations and spatial organization of such important turn-of-the-century railroad stations as Daniel Burnham's Union Station in Washington (1903–1907) and Union Station in New Orleans (1908), as well as Reed and Stem's New York Central Station in Troy,

Union Station, Troy, New York.

New York (1901–1904). Stations in Kansas City, Chattanooga, Detroit, and Toronto also emulated Atwood's scheme. The interior of McKim, Mead and White's Pennsylvania Station in New York was directly inspired by the baths of Caracalla in Rome. The main concourse of Grand Central does not recall such a specific model. Instead, its large, vaulted space is a metaphor of its prototype; while drawing on Roman bath design, it was a new creation.

□ The model for this spatial configuration, like that for the facade, has functional and contextual meaning for the building program. The Roman bath provides as a model a large, unobstructed space; as a place of public gathering, no better inspiration from the past could have been chosen. As much as its historicizing character, the plan and section of the terminal partake of ultimately the most influential aspect of Beaux-Arts design, its approach to planning and its conception of the design process. The terminal's symmetrical plan and particulate spaces are manifestations of the Beaux-Arts principle that such planning facilitates movement and ensures that the building will be functional and most practically expressive of its program. The Beaux-Arts philosophy insisted on the axial arrangement of space, with the creation of an enfilade, or succession of spaces, set along this axis. Whenever possible, circulation systems – that is, vestibules and hallways – should encircle the main space. Moving through Grand Central provides a lesson in the success of the Beaux-Arts method. The planning and circulation patterns of the building not only get us where we want to go with ease, but emphasize the drama of the most compelling space within – the main concourse.

□ The ramps running south-north along either side of the building bring us from 42nd Street to the main space; on the way another set of ramps intersects with the first, to take us, if we wish, to the lower level. If we take the middle doorway from 42nd Street, we pass through the main waiting room and down a ramped hallway to the concourse. In either case, the experience is one of passing through a relatively dark, low space into a bright, soaring space. It is a sensation of being pulled almost by the force of gravity toward a bustling room filled with the aura of romance surrounding people who are congregating in anticipation of travel, or moving swiftly toward another destination. If we enter from Vanderbilt Avenue, we experience the drama of seeing the great space from the level above.

□ What has been created here is a large public piazza for New York. Shops surround the concourse space on its periphery, people gather within it not only to wait for trains, but to meet other people, many use it as a city street, as a shortcut across town (particularly in bad weather), and all this happens with the "sky" above. For this was how the great public gathering space was intended to be experienced by its designer. Warren wrote, ". . .the up-to-date station resembles a bazaar. . . ."[17]

□ In the Paris of the 1880s, at the time when the young Whitney Warren was a student at the Ecole des Beaux-Arts, two design ideas were influential in architectural circles. The first, which was one chapter in an ongoing philosophical debate about the role of structure in the architectural aesthetics of the nineteenth century, was that the *actual* structure of a building need not be exaggerated or even made evident to the eye. French critics, and teachers at the Ecole, made an analogy between buildings and the human body: Just as the human skeleton was clothed, so should a building's skeleton or structure be concealed. The resonance of this idea is obvious in the design of Grand Central, where the entire supporting structure is made of steel, a fact that is hardly evident anywhere in the building – either by the structure being revealed or by its even being alluded to through composition or decoration. The building appears to be supported by traditional masonry construction. The only exceptions to this are in the use of the large windows, which imply a steel support system, and in an opening in the piers of the lower concourse, through which we can see the steel structure.

The second Parisian idea relates to the work and thought of Charles Garnier, architect of one of the era's most important buildings, the Paris Opera of 1861–1875. Garnier focused as much energy on the dynamics of social interaction as he did on his building's more utilitarian properties. Psychological and emotional requirements thus became part of the definition of a building's function. The opera's grand stairway not only leads us efficiently from the vestibule to the seats above, but it enables us to become part of our own theatrical spectacle as we watch and are watched by the operagoers in the galleries surrounding the stairway. A processional stairway, similar in dramatic function and almost a reverse in design of the opera model, is used by Warren in the main concourse of Grand Central.

Stairway, main concourse, Grand Central.

Grand Staircase, the Opéra, Paris.

In his 1871 book, *Le Théâtre*, Garnier described his design philosophy for the opera, "But what will be the dimensions of this foyer? To answer this question, one has to study the way people promenade."[18]

Whitney Warren's design for Grand Central displayed his affinity for French ideas. The terminal is designed as an area in which people can experience the romance and fantasy that are implicit in the idea of travel. Like Garnier, Warren was clearly responding to the emotional as well as the utilitarian needs of those who would use his building, both traveler and pedestrian. Embodied in the efficiency and the elegance that are Grand Central, it is the celebration of everyday life that continues to make the building mythologized and beloved for us.

1. Park Avenue first appears in the City Directory of 1860–1861 as the name applied to Fourth Avenue between 34th and 36th streets; Fourth Avenue was originally known as the upper end of Bowery Lane until 1817. By 1867 it was called Park Avenue up to 42nd Street, by 1888, as far north as 96th Street, and soon thereafter to the end of the island at the Harlem River. See Isaac Newton Phelps Stokes, **The Iconography of Manhattan Island**, 6 vols. (New York, 1915–1928), vol. 3, p. 1,000.

2. There have been four important publications on Grand Central Terminal: Carl W. Condit, **The Port of New York: A History of the Rail and Terminal System from the Grand Central Electrification to the Present**, 2 vols. (Chicago and London, 1980, 1981); James Marston Fitch and Diana S. Waite, **Grand Central Terminal and Rockefeller Center: A Historic-critical Estimate of Their Significance** (New York State Parks and Recreation, Division for Historic Preservation, 1974); David Marshall, **Grand Central** (New York, 1946); William Middleton, **Grand Central: the World's Greatest Railroad Terminal** (San Marino, California, 1977). By far the most thorough study, particularly in terms of technological information, is Condit's, which also includes a comprehensive bibliography, and has been an important source for the preparation of this essay. Fitch and Waite's volume is insightful for the architectural discussion of the terminal. Middleton's book provides valuable photographic material, an introduction to railroad history as it relates to Grand Central, and a general presentation of the development of the terminal. An important archival source for Grand Central is the William J. Wilgus Collection at The New York Public Library.

3. The Terminal City idea of a mixed-use complex of buildings was an inspiration for twentieth-century planners. The Rockefeller Center development is the most successful example of such a complex, in terms of function as well as design. For a thorough discussion of Rockefeller Center, see Carol Herselle Krinsky, **Rockefeller Center** (New York, 1978).

4. **Condit, Port of New York**, vol. 2, p. 9.

5. In 1980 terms the cost of replacing the terminal would be $1.6 billion. Ibid., p. 90.

6. Middleton, **Grand Central**, pp. 65, 66, connects the court of honor scheme with the original competition entry. Condit, **The Port of New York**, vol. 2, pp. 66 and 302 n. 16, suggests that it was developed after the competition was won. The latter is probably correct, as such an idea, in a specific physical form, is not developed by the other entrants.

7. For a detailed account of the American Renaissance style and the City Beautiful movement see Dianne H. Pilgrim, Richard N. Murray, Richard Guy Wilson, **The American Renaissance: 1876–1917** (New York, 1979) prepared in conjunction with an exhibition of the same name. See also Mel Scott, **American City Planning Since 1900** (Berkeley and Los Angeles, 1971).

8. The history of the move for such a plan is analyzed in Harvey A. Kantor, "The City Beautiful in New York," **The New-York Historical Society Quarterly** 67 (April 1973), pp. 148–171. My discussion is based primarily on this article.

9. "Would Make Grand Central a Public Monument," **The New York Times**, 15 March, 1903, p. 13.

10. Memorandum on Behalf of Plaintiff, The Supreme Court of New York County Trial before Justice Delahanty, January 27 to March 31, 1916, Allen Stem plaintiff against Whitney Warren and Charles D. Wetmore. The William Wilgus Collection, The New York Public Library, p. 6.

11. Photographs of this scheme are at Avery Library, Columbia University.

12. The competition was won and the building was designed by Cass Gilbert.

13. Helleu, who had studied in Paris with Gérôme, was best known for his portraits of the rich. The ceiling was executed by Charles Bassing of Brooklyn, New York. The fact that the constellations were reversed on the ceiling was discovered March 22, 1913, by a commuter from New Rochelle. **The New York Times** suggests that the reversal was due to Bassing's error. "Constellations Reversed: New Grand Central Ceiling Has the Heavens Turned Around," 23 March 1913, p. 10.

14. Among Coutan's works are the statue of Voltaire of 1882 at the City Hall in Paris, the caryatids of 1899 for the Opéra Comique in Paris; and the sculptural group of Military France on the Alexander III bridge in Paris. All other sculpture in the terminal was by Silvain Salieres. It is indicative of Warren's great love for French art and culture that he chose two conservative French artists for the most important ornamentation of the terminal.

15. This is an often-cited interpretation by Whitney Warren, made on the occasion of the opening of the terminal in 1913. See Middleton, **Grand Central**, p. 72.

16. Carroll L. V. Meeks, **The Railroad Station** (New Haven, 1956). This book is an important history of the building type. For a discussion of Atwood's contribution to late 19th-century station architecture, see p. 128.

17. **The New York Times**, 9 February 1913, section 6, p. 9.

18. As quoted in David Van Zanten, "Architectural Composition at the Ecole des Beaux-Arts from Charles Percier to Charles Garnier," Arthur Drexler, ed., **The Architecture of the Ecole des Beaux-Arts**, (Cambridge, Mass., 1977), p. 232. The Van Zanten essay provides the background for this discussion of Parisian architectural ideas in the last decades of the 19th century.

Grand Central Depot

Grand Central Depot, constructed 1869-1871. Forty-second Street facade.
Architect: John B. Snook. Photograph circa 1893.

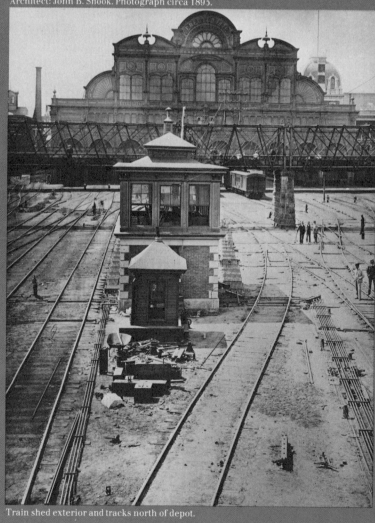

Train shed exterior and tracks north of depot.

Grand Central Depot train shed under construction.

Grand Central Depot train shed interior.

Grand Central Depot, Vanderbilt Avenue facade. Drawing by John B. Snook.

Grand Central Station after 1899.

In 1898 a new facade was erected around the 42nd Street depot and three stories were added. Architect: Bradford L. Gilbert. In 1900 the interior was remodeled to combine separate waiting rooms into one. Architect: Samuel Huckel, Jr.

Grand Central Station waiting room after 1900.

Postcard view of Grand Central Station.

Postcard with cut-away showing the route of the IRT subway (completed in 1904) as it turned west on 42nd Street.

McKim, Mead and White competition entry, 42nd Street facade.

McKim, Mead and White competition entry, Park Avenue facade.

In 1903 the New York Central and Hudson River Railroad organized a limited competition for the design of a new terminal on 42nd Street to replace the existing building. The architectural firm of Reed and Stem won the competition.

Reed and Stem competition entry, 42nd Street facade.

Reed and Stem design for a "Court of Honor" on Park Avenue north of the terminal. Competition entry or subsequent proposal, 1903.

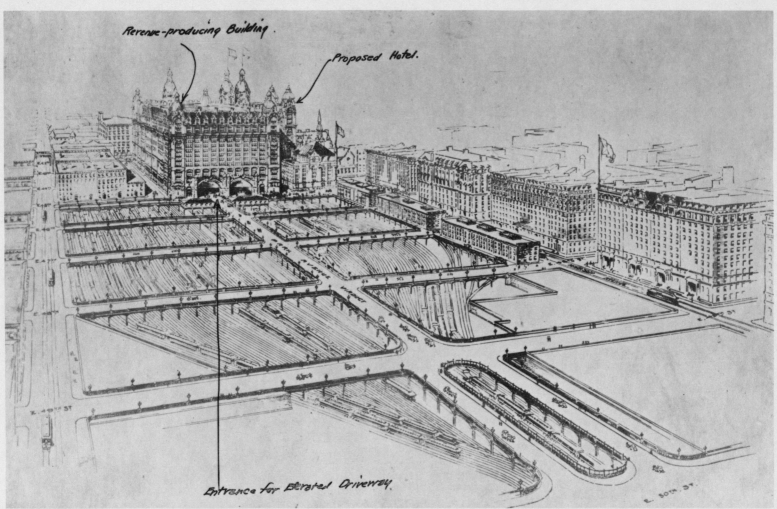

Samuel Huckel, Jr. competition entry, Park Avenue facade.

Warren and Wetmore scheme, dated 1903, redated 1904.

After the commission for the terminal
was awarded to Reed and Stem, the firm
of Warren and Wetmore proposed its
own scheme, and eventually
collaborated with Reed and Stem on the
design of the terminal.

Warren and Wetmore scheme, 42nd Street facade, dated 1903, redated 1904.

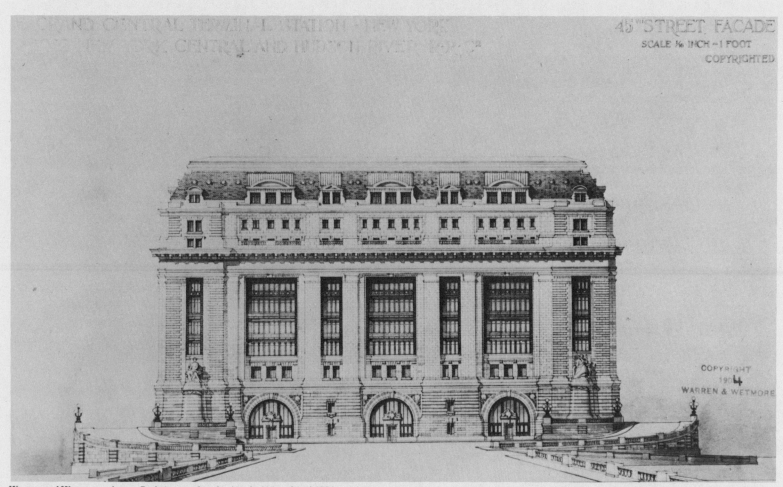

Warren and Wetmore scheme, Park Avenue facade, dated 1903, redated 1904.

The Design of Grand Central Terminal, 1905-1910

Scheme of 1905. *Scientific American*, December 9, 1905.

Scheme of 1906. *The Inland Architect*, February 1906.

Scheme of 1907. Drawn by Vernon Howe Bailey. *Harper's Weekly*, January 1907.

Study drawing for the 42nd Street
facade, from the office of Warren and
Wetmore, with notes by Whitney
Warren. March 1, 1910.

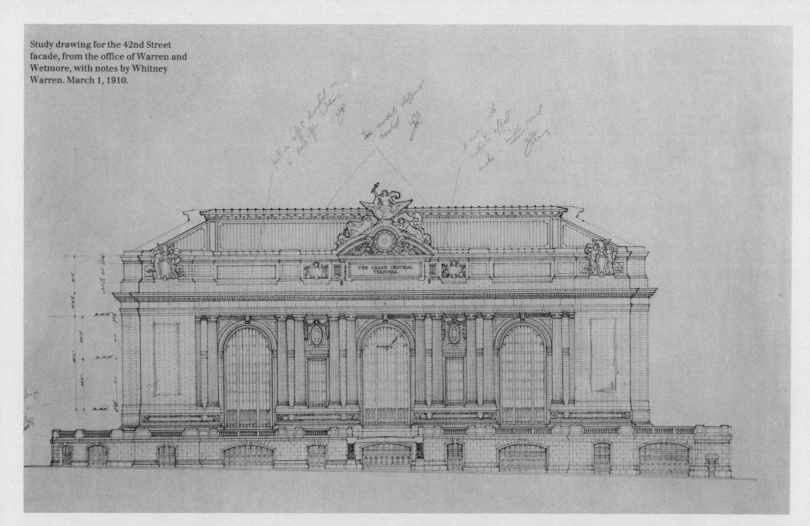

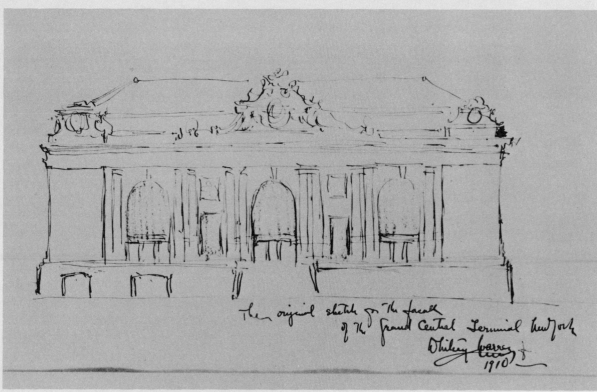

Sketch of 1910 by Whitney Warren for the 42nd Street facade.

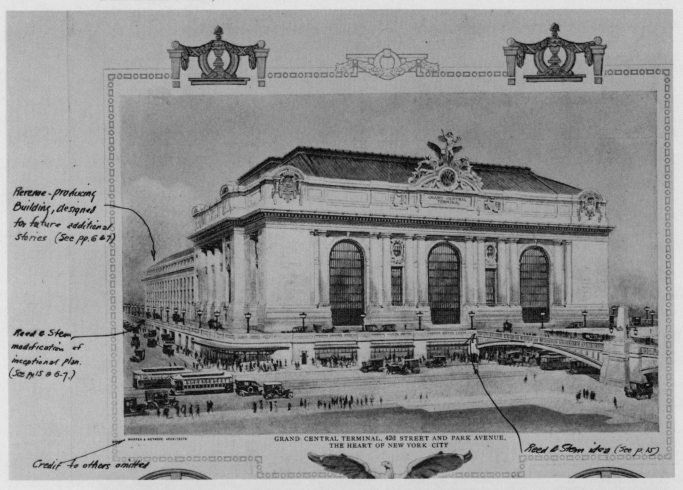

Revenue-producing
Building, designed
for future additional
stories (See pp. 6 & 7)

Reed & Stem
modification of
inceptional plan.
(See pp. 15 & 6-7.)

GRAND CENTRAL TERMINAL, 42d STREET AND PARK AVENUE,
THE HEART OF NEW YORK CITY

WARREN & WETMORE, ARCHITECTS

Reed & Stem idea (See p. 15)

Credit to others omitted

Model of the 42nd Street facade of Grand Central Terminal.

Proposal for skyscraper
over Grand Central, con-
ceived before 1913.

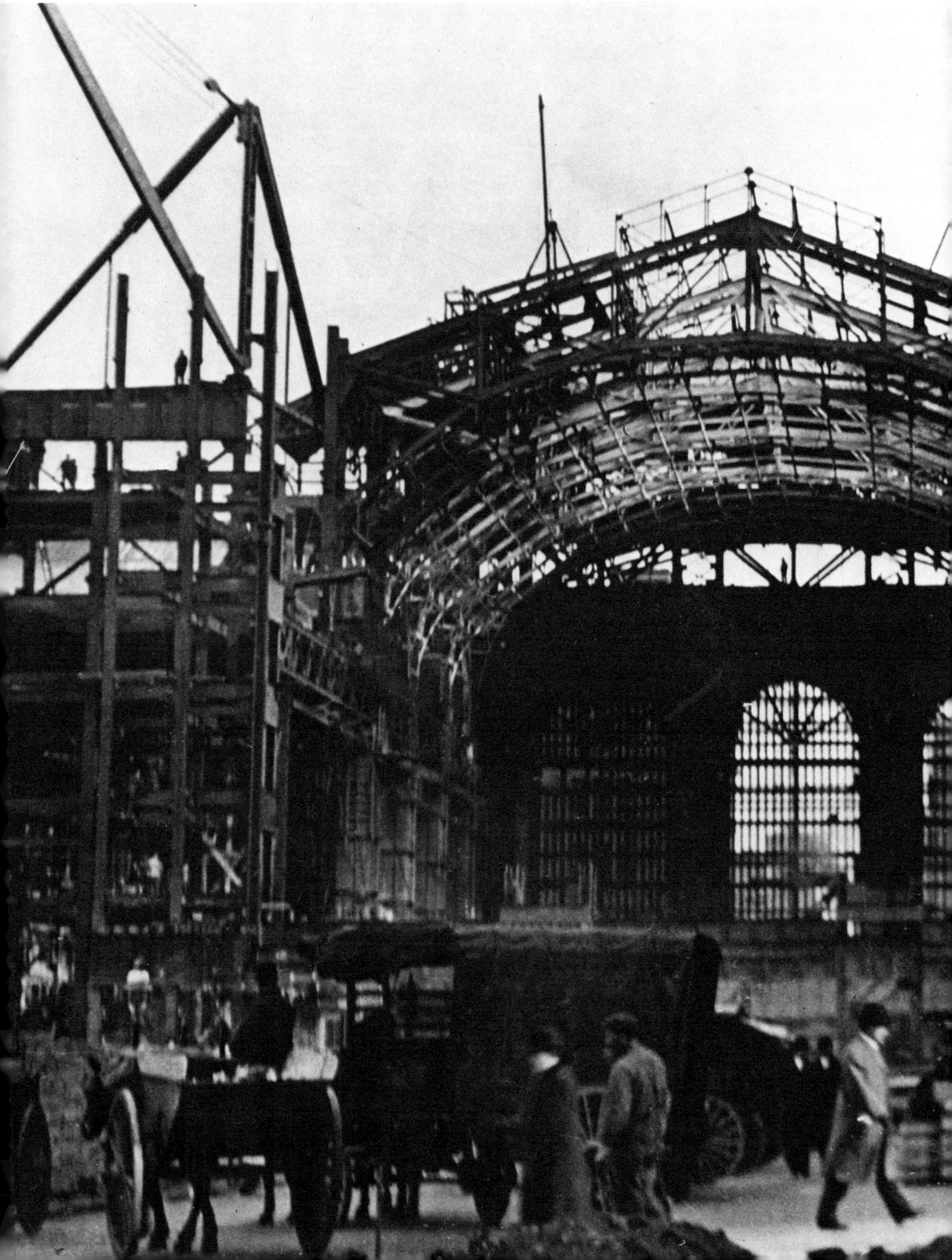

Grand Central Terminal under
construction, showing steel structure
and stone cladding, circa 1912.

Section of Grand Central Terminal, *Scientific American*, December 7, 1912.

Grand Central Terminal,
main concourse.

Main concourse, entrance to express trains.

Drawing of the ceiling of
the main concourse.

Ceiling of main
concourse.

fold out

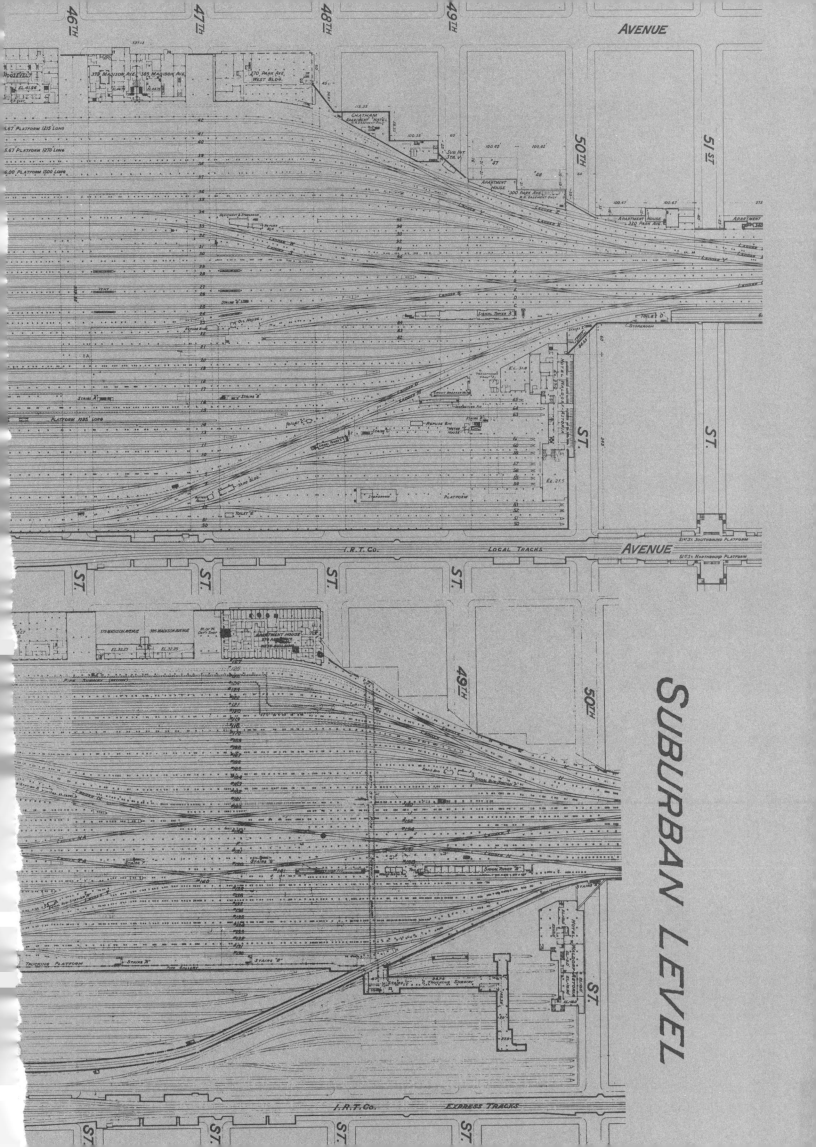

SUBURBAN LEVEL

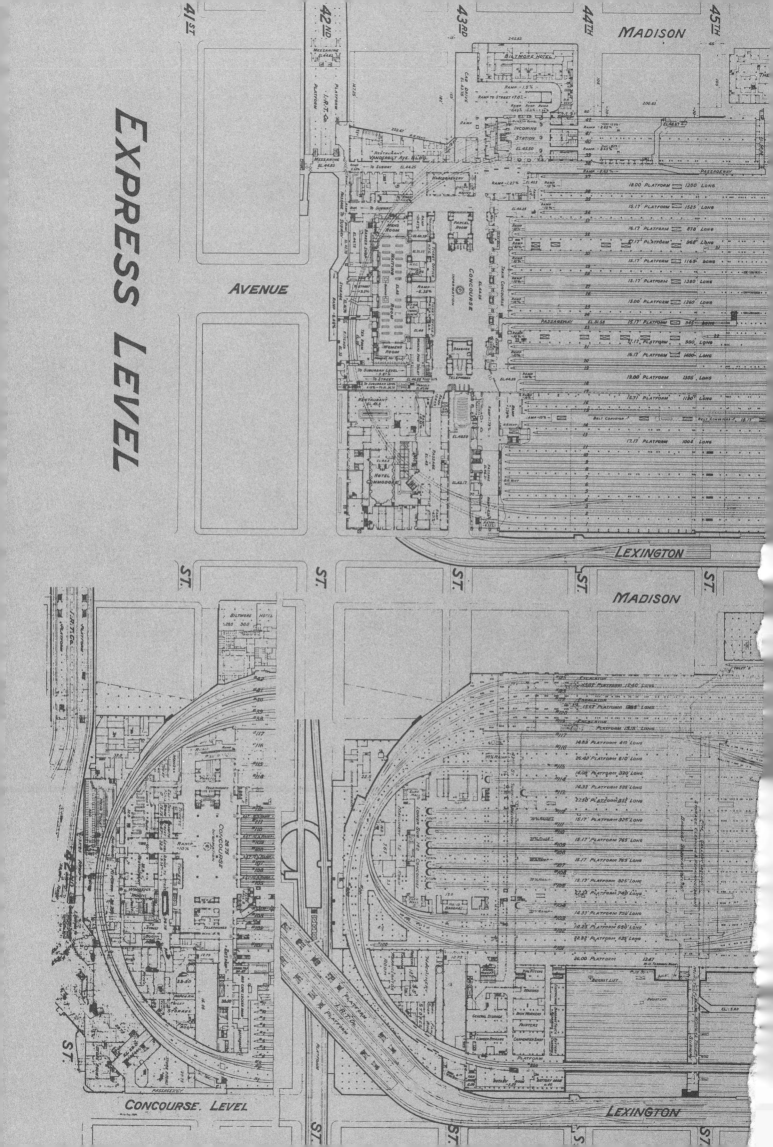

EXPRESS LEVEL

CONCOURSE LEVEL

Detail of walls and ceiling in main concourse.

Stairs leading from
Vanderbilt Avenue to
main concourse.

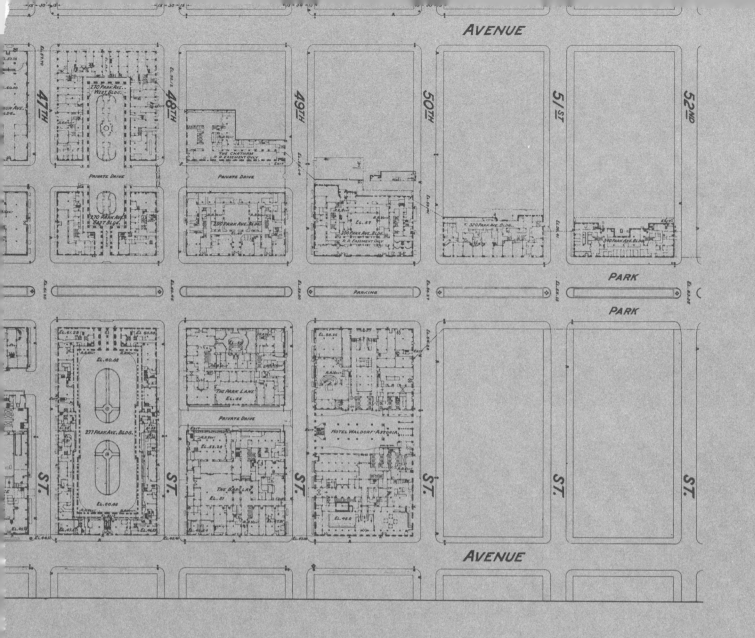

N.Y.C.R.R.
GRAND CENTRAL TERMINAL
NEW YORK CITY
STREET LEVEL

SCALE

NEW YORK, OCT. 1, 1931. REVISED: 7-24-52

OFFICE OF CHIEF ENGINEER.

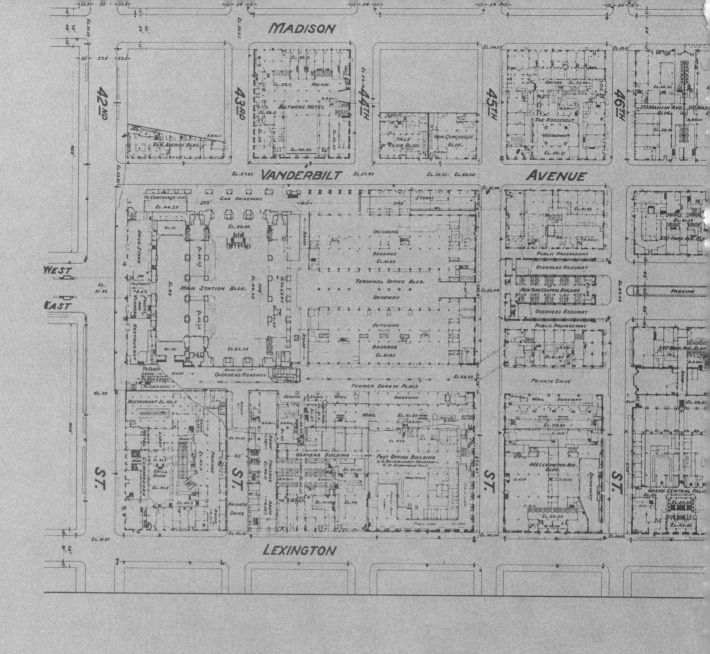

Main waiting room.

Suburban train level.

Interior, Oyster Bar
Restaurant.

Section of Jules Coutan's statue of Mercury before placement on the terminal's 42nd Street facade, March 1914.

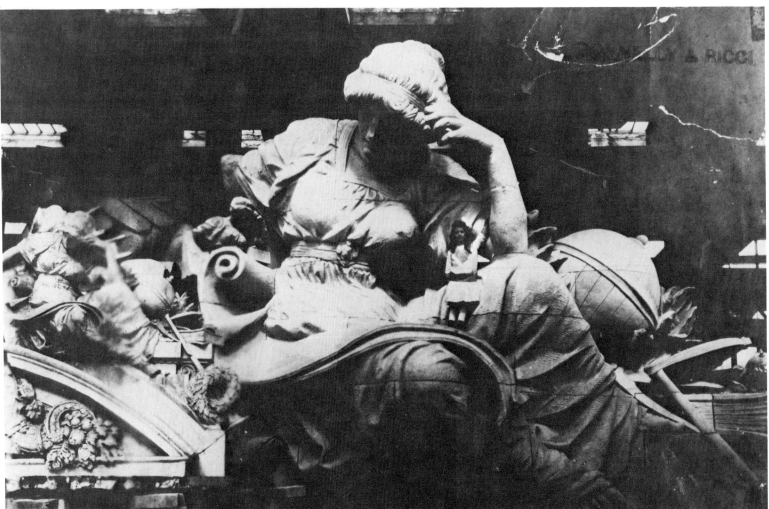

Coutan's statue of Minerva and maquettes of statue, photographed in the studio of Donnelly and Ricci.

Installing the statue of
Mercury, Hercules, and
Minerva on the 42nd
Street facade of Grand
Central Terminal, 1914.

To J. Pierpont Morgan
Whitney Warren
11 July 1914
The last stone of
the Grand Central
Terminal

Grand Central Terminal, 42nd Street facade, 1914.

Grand Central Terminal, 1934.

Grand Central Terminal,
main concourse, 1930s.

Grand Central Terminal,
42nd Street facade, 1978.

51

New York Central Glee Club performing in the gallery above the main concourse.

Armistice Day, the main concourse.

Coco Chanel on the 20th Century Limited, Grand Central Terminal.

Dwight D. Eisenhower at Grand Central Terminal.

Winston Churchill at Grand Central Terminal.

Park Avenue
North of 42nd Street, 1836-1907

Blasting the tunnel for
tracks at 90th Street and
Fourth Avenue for the
New York & Harlem
Railroad, circa 1836.

Park Avenue at 96th
Street, looking
northwest, circa 1885-86.
Holes to emit steam from
the railroad tunnel are
visible.

Railroad tracks between 98th-112th streets, looking north, circa 1880.

View of "beam tunnel" from 59th to 76th streets, looking north on Fourth Avenue. *Frank Leslie's Illustrated Newspaper*, February 15, 1873.

Train shed, Grand Central Depot. *Frank Leslie's Illustrated Newspaper*, November 26, 1870.

Park Avenue at 34th Street. Unitarian Church of the Messiah at the northwest corner of Park Avenue and 34th Street.

Park Avenue, looking north from 32nd Street, circa 1875. The Park Avenue Hotel is on the west side of the street. Grand Central Depot is barely visible in the far distance.

Park Avenue and Grand Central Depot from 41st Street, before 1886.

Looking north on Park Avenue from 40th Street. The Murray Hill Hotel, opened in 1884, is on the west side of Park Avenue between 40th and 41st streets.

61

Forty-second Street Before 1900.

Looking east on 42nd
Street from Fifth Avenue
towards Grand Central
Depot, circa 1881.

Forty-second Street, looking west from Park Avenue, after 1886.

West 42nd Street, looking east from Sixth Avenue, 1876.

Looking east on 42nd Street.

Forty-second Street After 1900

East 42nd Street, looking
west from Park Avenue,
with Grand Central
Station on the right.

East 42nd Street, looking west from Vanderbilt Avenue, May 1, 1903. IRT subway, to be opened in 1904, under construction.

Park Avenue and Grand Central Depot
from 41st Street, before 1886.

The Hotel Belmont will
be constructed on the
site of the Park Avenue
Oyster House opposite
Grand Central (Hotel
Belmont: see photograph
to the right).

Hotel Belmont, southwest
corner of 42nd Street and
Park Avenue, opened
1906, demolished 1931.

A — 42d St. and Fifth Ave. — Neal, Florist — Lyons, Umbrellas — Edwin B. Willcox, Real Estate — Wolff & Co., Bicycles — 503 5th Ave., Wm. R. Rowland, Real Estate — 1 E. 42d, Willie Dunn, Golf Links — 3 E. 42d, F. H. Warner, Furnishings — 5 E. 42d, Angus Tavern, Cafe — 9 E. 42d, Geo. N. Pierce & Co., Bicycles — 11 E. 42d, F. G. Schmidt, Optician — Madison Ave. & 42d, Manhattan Hotel, 17 Stories High

MADISON AVENUE. VANDERBILT AVENUE.

B — Madison Ave. & 42d, F. K. Tripler & Co., Gents Furnisher — 17 E. 42d, John Nicholas, Florist — 39 E. 42d, S. A. MacFarland & Co., Statuary and Granit — 41 E. 42d, Fox, Optician — 43 E. 42d, Levy & Stream, Cigars — 47 E. 42d, Betts' Restaurant — 49 E. 42d, White, Van Glahn & Co., Hardware — 51 E. 42d, Mendel Candies — 42d St. & Vanderbilt Ave., James A. Hetherington, Druggist

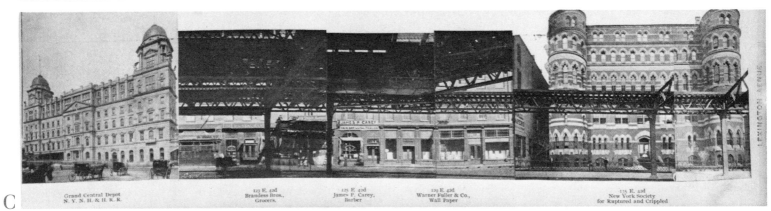

LEXINGTON AVENUE

C — Grand Central Depot, N. Y., N. H. & H. R. R. — 123 E. 42d, Brandess Bros., Grocers — 125 E. 42d, James P. Carey, Barber — 129 E. 42d, Warner Fuller & Co., Wall Paper — 125 E. 42d, New York Society for Ruptured and Crippled

D — 127 E. 42d, H. A. Sohl, Stationery — 129 E. 42d, Grand Central Hotel — 131 E. 42d, McCarthy's Hotel — 159 E. 42d, Transfer Hotel Restaurant — 161 E. 42d, J. F. Jahrans, Barber — 3d Ave. & 42d, Henry Bohufalk, Druggist

Forty-second Street, 1900

70

ROBERT BURNS CIGARS

MADISON AVENUE.

FIFTH AVENUE.

26 E. 42d
Grace & Hyde Co.,
Contractors & Builders
Henry A. Hagan Decorator

24 E. 42d
J. J. Mackeown
Spectacles

22 E. 42d
Yonkers Park
& Hollwood
C. Just & Co. Cigars

16 E. 42d
Dr. H. Willcox,
Dentist

14 E. 42d
The Park
Men's Belongings

12 E. 42d
Robertson Bros.,
Art Stationers

8 E. 42d
Richard Gledhill,
Wall Paper & Decorator

5th Ave. & 42d
American
Safe Deposit Building

E

HOTEL DEVONSHIRE

BARBER TRUCKS

A. HANK

MADISON AVENUE.

38 E. 42d
Lincoln Safe Deposit Co.

32 E. 42d
Hotel Devonshire

24 E. 42d

24 E. 42d
A. Hank
Jeweler

26½ E. 42d
Wenham
Florist

24 E. 42d
L. F. Gondolfo
Fruiterer

Madison Ave. & 42d
Decker & St. John
Cigars

F

PARK AVENUE.

F. W. SCHOONMAKER,

PERPENTE and CLARKE
HABERDASHERS

RESTAURANT. TRUNKS & BAGS.

F. A. CAUCHOIS & CO.

Park Ave. & 42d
F. W. Schoonmaker
Pharmacy

Providence Saving-
Loan Ins. Co.

48 E. 42d
Perpente & Clarke
Shirt Makers

46 E. 42d
Polymero & R'ngar
Restaurant

44 E. 42d
J. J. Schoff
Trunks

42 E. 42d
Grand Central
Lunch

40 E. 42d
F. A. Cauchois & Co.
Groceries

38 E. 42d
Lincoln Safe Deposit Co.

G

LEXINGTON AVENUE.

PARK AVENUE.

Lexington Ave. & 42d
Manhattan Storage

42d St. Car Barn and Stables

Park Ave. & 42d
Grand Union Hotel

H

THIRD AVENUE.

CHARLES CONNER

GEO. EBRETT'S EXTRA BEER

TABLE D'HOTE WITH WINE

ENGRAVERS THOS. F. EAGAN & SON

3d Ave. & 42d
Charles Conner
Café

162 E. 42d
Kiley Express

160 E. 42d   158 E. 42d

156 E. 42d

152 & 154 E. 42d
Sherman Hotel
& Restaurant

148 E. 42d
T. F. Eagan & Son
Engravers

I

Terminal City and the Development of Park Avenue, 1903-1931

Rendering of Grand Central Terminal with proposal for the "air rights" development of buildings over its trackage. The scheme was called The Terminal City. The Commodore Hotel at 43rd Street and Vanderbilt Avenue is on the left. *Scientific American*, December 7, 1912.

Rendering looking south on Park Avenue showing trackage and location of air rights sites. *Scientific American*, December 7, 1912.

Excavation of Park Avenue north of Grand Central during construction of trackage for terminal, looking north.

Excavation of Park Avenue north of Grand Central during construction of trackage for terminal, looking south.

Excavation of Park Avenue north of Grand Central during construction of trackage for terminal, looking south.

Park Avenue, looking
north from 45th Street,
November 25, 1913. The
median of Park Avenue is
already ornamented by a
lattice-work design,
signifying that the street
was seen from the first as
a boulevard of very
special importance and
elegance worthy of
decoration. The Grand
Central Palace is seen on
the far right.

Panoramic view of Park
Avenue, looking south
from 50th Street toward
the terminal, circa 1913.

The Grand Central Palace.

This apartment house on Park Avenue was typical of the elegant detailing and scale of the buildings constructed on the terminal's air rights property during the late teens and 1920s.

Park Avenue, looking north from 50th Street, 1929. The central strip on Park Avenue is rectangular, as it is today.

Park Avenue, looking south from 50th Street, circa 1907.

Park Avenue, looking south from 56th Street, circa 1927. In 1917 the median strip was redesigned and acquired the undulating form of the planting areas that created a park-like image appropriate to the name of the street. In 1927 the plantings were laid out in rectangular form.

Aerial view looking south down Park Avenue from the 50s, 1931. The buildings on the air rights sites have been completed, and Park Avenue has become an enclave of elegant apartment houses, hotels, and offices. The Waldorf-Astoria, the Chrysler building, the RCA building, and St. Bartholomew's are to the left. The New York Central Building has just been completed and forms a closure to upper Park Avenue.

Park Avenue, looking
north from 38th Street,
1928. Park Avenue below
the terminal retained its
turn-of-the-century
quality until after World
War II.

Madison Avenue and 42nd Street, southwest corner.

Madison Avenue and 42nd Street, southwest corner, 1920s.

Airlines Terminal Building, 1939, 42nd Street facade.

Construction site of the
Airlines Terminal
Building, 42nd Street and
Park Avenue, now the
site of the headquarters
of Philip Morris
Incorporated.

Hotel Belmont.
Later the site of the
Airlines Terminal
Building.

Aerial view East 42nd Street, 1930s.

Grand Central Terminal and Park Avenue (photograph–1970s).

Park Avenue north of Grand Central Terminal (photograph–1970s).

Grand Central Terminal area, 1981.

As the midtown Manhattan area surrounding Grand Central Station continues its dynamic development, the presence of a superb new office tower is particularly welcome. Grand Central Tower stands only 538 feet from the Terminal itself; a handsome masonry and glass tower, with a 100-foot wide plaza and soaring three-story atrium running from 44th to 45th Streets.

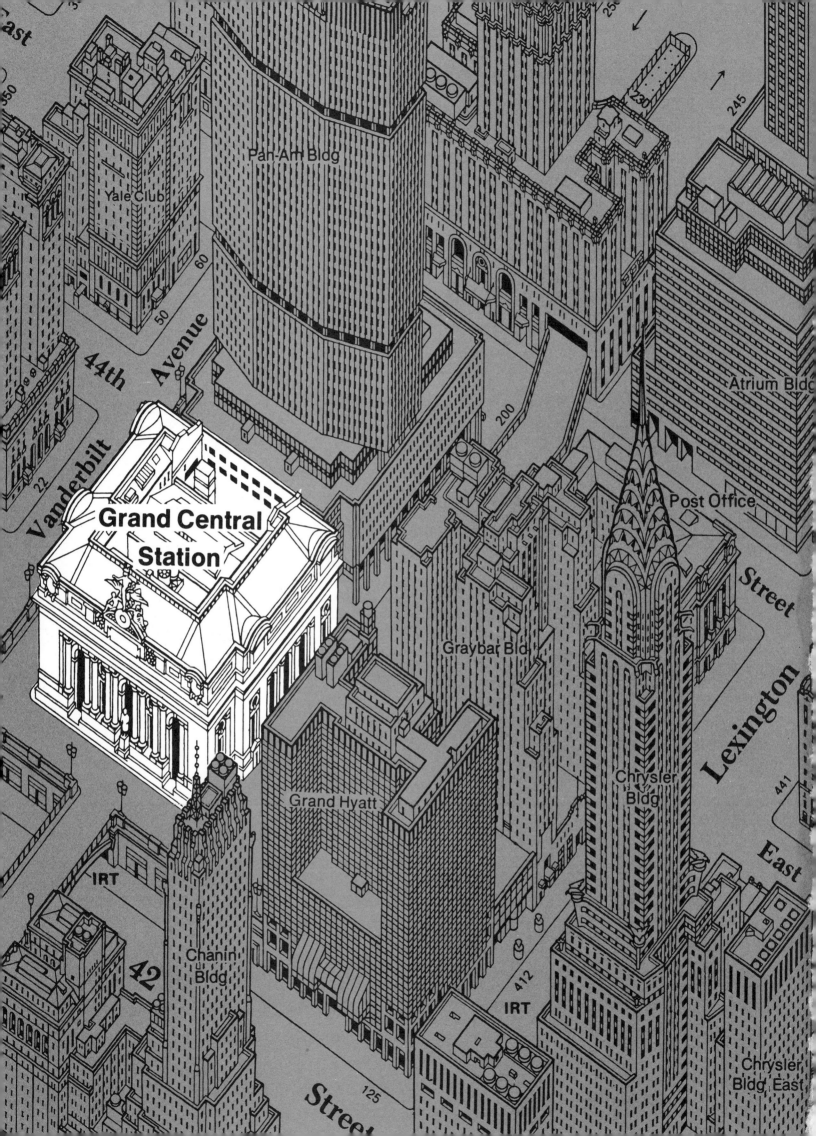

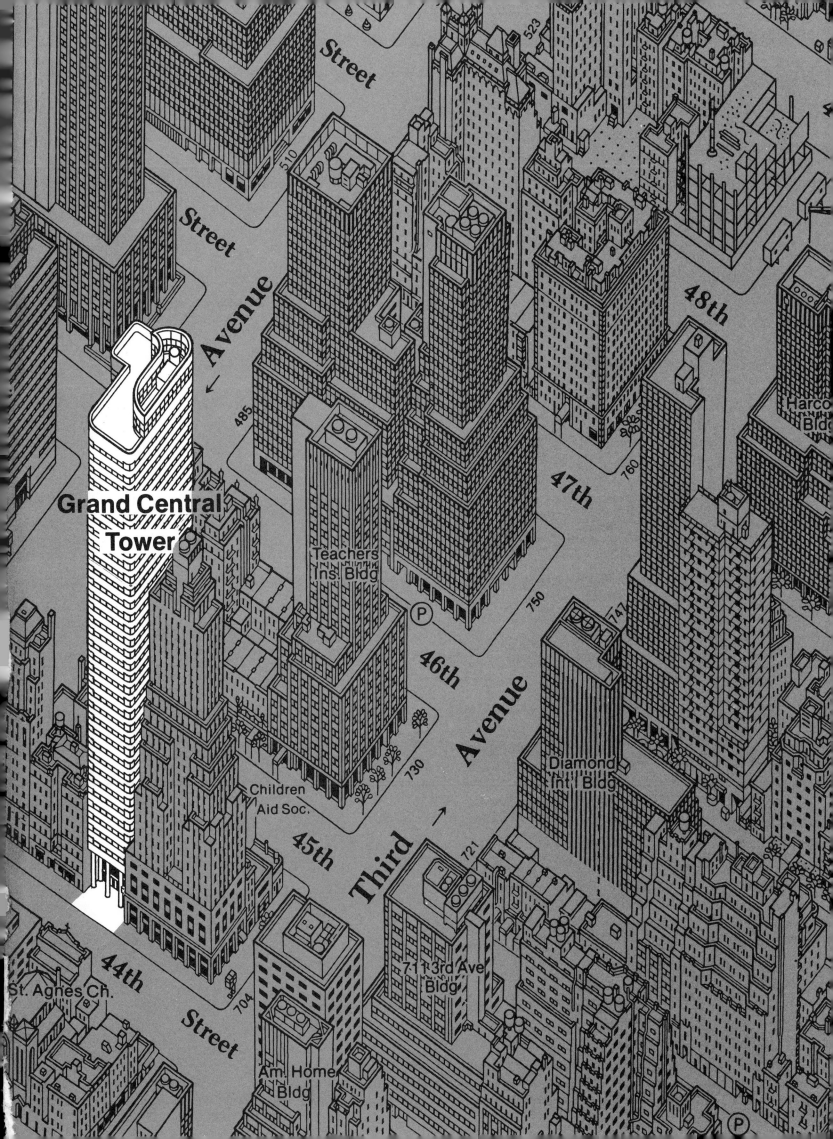

Grand Central Tower

Teachers Ins Bldg

Children Aid Soc.

St. Agnes Ch.

71 3rd Ave Bldg

Am. Home Bldg

Diamond Int'l Bldg

Harco Bldg

Street

Avenue

48th

47th

46th

45th

44th

Third Avenue

Street

Street

510

485

730

704

721

750

760

747

523

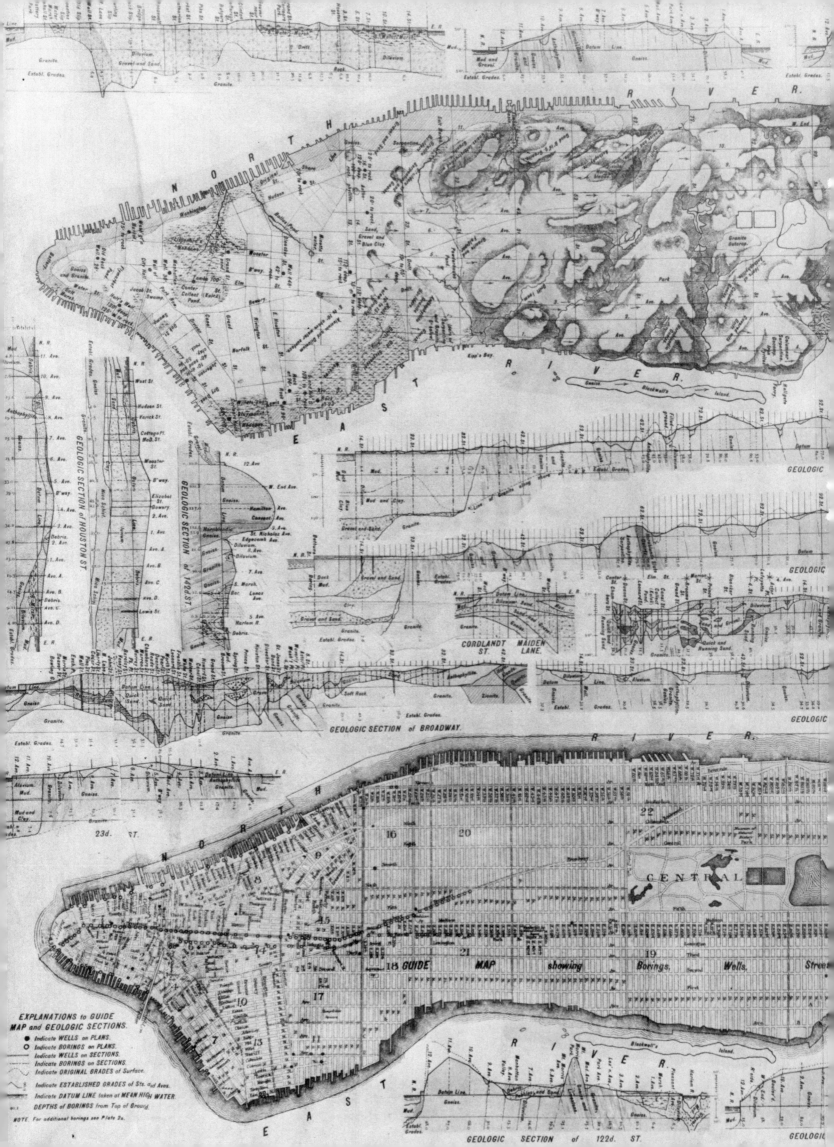

GEOLOGIC SECTION of HOUSTON ST.

GEOLOGIC SECTION of 140d ST.

GEOLOGIC SECTION of BROADWAY.

CORDLANDT ST. MAIDEN LANE.

GUIDE MAP showing Borings, Wells, Streets

CENTRAL

EXPLANATIONS to GUIDE MAP and GEOLOGIC SECTIONS.

- ● Indicate WELLS on PLANS.
- ○ Indicate BORINGS on PLANS.
- Indicate WELLS on SECTIONS.
- Indicate BORINGS on SECTIONS.
- Indicate ORIGINAL GRADES of Surface.
- Indicate ESTABLISHED GRADES of Sts. and Aves.
- Indicate DATUM LINE taken at MEAN HIGH WATER.
- DEPTHS of BORINGS from Top of Ground.

NOTE. For additional borings see Plate 2a.

GEOLOGIC SECTION of 122d. ST.

Elliot Willensky

■ The future of commercial, residential, and industrial Manhattan was to be inordinately influenced by the completion in 1871 of the first and now-vanished Grand Central, the enormous train depot built on 42nd Street's north side, straddling the axis of what was then referred to as "the Fourth Avenue." Commodore Vanderbilt's new rococo structure succeeded in giving New York both a properly ornate gateway for incoming passengers and a place of convenient accessibility to points as far west as the Pacific coast – via the transcontinental service begun the previous year. The elaborately embellished passenger depot, the great arched train shed it shielded from the environs to the west and south, and the fan of tracks that fed the complex all joined to create an immense intrusion in the neat gridiron plan of avenues and streets that had been established back in 1811 to channel Manhattan's growth. This intrusion, which in 1871 was hardly a serious problem in an area still rife with vacant lots, was to become a consequential one as the city grew inevitably northward, enveloping the site of the depot and its yards. The 1913 Grand Central Terminal we know today occupies that same site, much expanded.

Manhattan's early boundaries—since extended by fill—and its irregular topography are here contrasted with the neatness of the later gridiron street plan in this detail from *Geological Map and Sections of Manhattan Island*, prepared in 1898 by Leonard E. Graether.

□ By cutting off the cross streets above 42nd Street and stopping the north-south flow of the thoroughfare which would be renamed Park Avenue, the depot's vast acreage interrupted the natural evolution of the crazy quilt created by Manhattan's real estate speculation. It also produced a physical separation between the dense working-class tenement

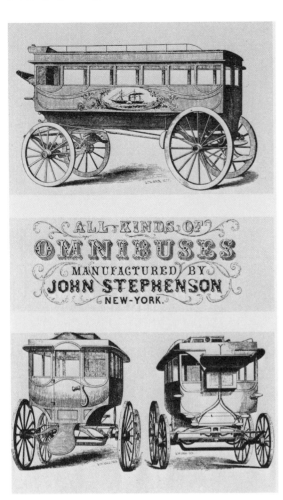

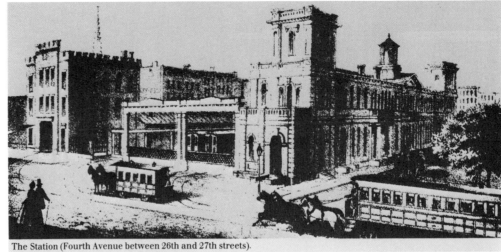

The Station (Fourth Avenue between 26th and 27th streets).

CARS TAKING ENGINE FROM NEW YORK TO BOSTON.

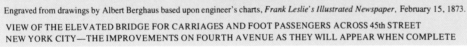

Engraved from drawings by Albert Berghaus based upon engineer's charts, *Frank Leslie's Illustrated Newspaper*, February 15, 1873.

VIEW OF THE ELEVATED BRIDGE FOR CARRIAGES AND FOOT PASSENGERS ACROSS 45th STREET
NEW YORK CITY—THE IMPROVEMENTS ON FOURTH AVENUE AS THEY WILL APPEAR WHEN COMPLETE

ELEVATED BRIDGE FOR FOOT PASSENGERS
BETWEEN 52d AND 53d STREETS

THE STONE VIADUCT FROM 99th TO 115th STREET—
THE STATION AT 110th STREET

The Grand Central Depot, 42nd Street and Fourth Avenue.

From *Frank Leslie's Illustrated Newspaper*, November 26, 1870.

FOR THE NEW YORK CENTRAL AND HUDSON RIVER AND NEW HAVEN AND HARLEM RAILROADS,
FOURTH AVENUE, NEW YORK CITY

developments to its east and the genteel refinements of Fifth and Madison avenues to its west. And through a combination of the railroad-owned properties surrounding it and the devaluation of adjacent plots because of the smoke and cinders and sounds of steam locomotives, the depot established a land bank for New York's future.

□ Both Grand Centrals – the original of 1871 and its 1913 replacement – were to act as spatial and temporal modulators of Manhattan's development. The greatly expanded site of the terminal's yards would become a major resource for larger scaled development – not once, but twice – over the next fifty years. As a nineteenth-century phenomenon that encouraged and shaped the form Manhattan would take in the twentieth, Grand Central also enriched and enlivened the city's second business district, the enclave it had attracted to its surrounds, midtown. Indeed, it would be impossible to account for the growth of midtown without the decision to build the original Grand Central where today's terminal stands.

□ What was the city like before there was a Grand Central?

□ The 1820 census had clearly demonstrated New York's primacy over Philadelphia as the nation's most populous city. Until the 1830s the city's population was concentrated in the half-square-mile of Manhattan's toe. But now New York was to emerge from two centuries of contained settlement, and an era during which work and residence were located cheek by jowl would end. With evidence of a growing commercial affluence and a population that would triple every thirty years between 1820 and 1910, the city would clearly have to occupy new lands to the north on its long, narrow island, bounded east and west by major waterways not to be surmounted, except by ferry, for at least sixty years. The pedestrian could prevail no longer; the journey to work would now have to be accomplished by some sort of wheeled transportation. The key to the city's expansion would lie in developing as yet untried forms of public conveyance and in the workability of the street plan that had been enacted in 1811 to guide the city's future advance northward.

□ The 1811 Commissioners Plan for New York City had set forth the series of wide avenues running parallel to Manhattan's lengthwise axis and the mix of narrow and wide streets running crosswise, river to river – the arrangement that is commonly referred to today as the gridiron plan. Into that regularly spaced grid, the state legislature in the early 1830s first added Irving Place and Lexington Avenue, between the

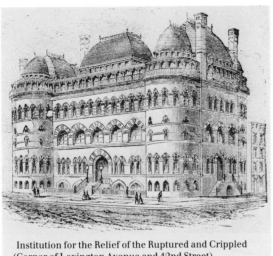

Institution for the Relief of the Ruptured and Crippled
(Corner of Lexington Avenue and 42nd Street)

Rutgers Female College
(Fifth Avenue and 41st Street)

Jewish Temple
(Fifth Avenue, corner of 43rd Street)

Engraved from a drawing by W. P. Snyder, *Harper's Weekly*, July 20, 1878.

THE FORTY-SECOND STREET AND SIXTH AVENUE STATION, METROPOLITAN (GILBERT) ELEVATED RAILWAY

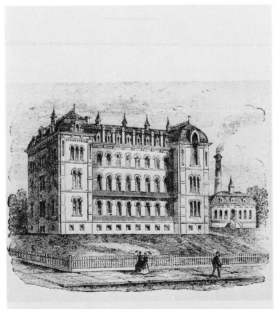

The Woman's Hospital of the State of New York
(Fourth Avenue and 50th Street)

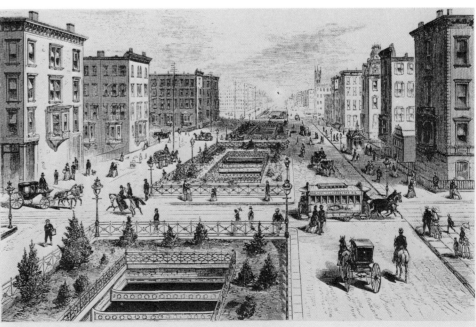

VIEW OF THE BEAM TUNNEL FROM 59th TO 76th STREET, LOOKING NORTH

lines of Third and Fourth avenues, and later added Madison Avenue, between Fourth and Fifth.[1] Though these thoroughfares were planned initially to run for only a few dozen blocks, their addition to the grid inevitably added an impetus to north-south movement patterns along Manhattan's east flank which could do nothing but grow as the city itself grew. In short order, Samuel B. Ruggles, the developer of Gramercy Park and its adjacent lands, built Irving Place and Lexington Avenue at his own expense.[2] Ruggles, in addition to being a real estate developer, was also interested in the potentialities of the railroad at a time when the city had barely even become aware of its first form of rapid transit, the omnibus.

□ Long-distance intercity stage coaches to Philadelphia and Boston were well established by 1830, and intermediate-length routes from Wall Street to the outlying villages of Yorkville, Harlem, and Manhattanville had existed since about 1803,[3] but the concept of local public conveyances traveling short distances over fixed routes and stopping at every opportunity for a paying passenger was an unfamiliar one until 1829. In that year, Abraham Brower introduced such a service in the form of a four-wheeled, horse-drawn stage-coach of sorts which he called, appropriately, *Accommodation*. The idea caught on and within the year he added another, *Sociable*.[4] By 1834 more than a hundred such vehicles plied the streets, leading a local journal to dub New York "The City of Omnibuses."[5] As popular as omnibuses seemed to be becoming, they weren't comfortable.[6] At the least, the irregularity of the city's street surfaces made for bumpy rides, and the shape of the coaches offered limited headroom for standees. In later years it would be said that "Modern martyrdom may be succinctly defined as riding in a New York omnibus."[7] When metal rails were substituted for the irregular street surfaces used by the omnibus, the ride would be smoother, and the reduced friction and improved adhesion meant that the coaches could be larger and go faster.

□ New York City's first railroad, the New York & Harlem Railroad Company, chartered in 1831, became a reality in 1832 with the introduction of a horse-drawn streetcar line – America's first – from Prince Street north along the Bowery and lower Fourth Avenue up to Union Square at 14th Street.[8] This route, however, was only incidental to the more ambitious plans of the New York & Harlem's incorporators: a route extending up what the 1811 Commissioners Plan called the Fourth Avenue (known today as Park Avenue, its lower part called Park Avenue South). The holders of the railroad's charter had actually planned a suburban commuter line, to link their produce mart at Fourth Avenue between 27th and 28th streets with the prosperous village of Harlem, five miles to the north, where a number of them enjoyed real estate interests.[9]

□ The intervening landscape along the route was a difficult one, with hills that would one day assume the names Murray, Lenox, and Carnegie; the existing stage routes wandered to and fro to avoid these natural obstructions. But despite the quality of the abstraction called Fourth Avenue – it was visible

only on the official city maps downtown, and to a small degree in Harlem, where its surface had been laid down by local landowners – the railroad stuck to its approved straight-as-an-arrow route. Why shouldn't it? The company had, through its charter and local ordinances, wangled for its own use a free, twenty-four-foot-wide strip of land that ran up the spine of Manhattan.

□ Doggedly, over the next five years, a pathway of track was placed northward through open country along the line of future Fourth Avenue, into cuts, over fill, through a tunnel blasted from Manhattan's rock, and across a timber viaduct. By 1833 horses were drawing passenger cars up to 32nd Street, by 1834 to 85th Street. At last, in late 1837, it was possible to take a trip, using a combination of horses and steam locomotives,[10] between the city – which still lay below Union Square – and Harlem. The changeover from horses to steam power took place at the New York & Harlem's first real station, built on the west side of Fourth Avenue between 26th and 27th streets, across from the railroad's earlier produce market and cater corner to Madison Square. It was at this station that the horse-drawn streetcars of the railroad terminated their run, to be replaced by the admired, feared, and noisome steam locomotives that would continue the trek northward; they had been banished from the populous city to the south by the concerns of the city's Common Council.[11]

□ With a horsecar line extending from the Bowery to their Madison Square station, and a steam line completed to Harlem, the railroad's owners looked beyond their charter, limited to Manhattan Island, to opportunities across the narrow Harlem River, opportunities that would link the New York & Harlem with the mainland of North America. A connection to the upstate New York industries of Troy-Watervliet-Albany as well as to those of western Massachusetts looked appealing. Conveniently, the same year that marked the completion of the route to Harlem also saw the financial panic of 1837. One of its victims, the projected New York & Albany Railroad, gave the Harlem the chance it needed. It bought the ill-fated line's bargain-priced right-of-way, broadened its own charter to permit northward expansion, and, by 1840, struck out for a connection to Albany, Pittsfield, and Springfield via an inland route that took it through today's Chatham, New York.

□ The fierce competition by Hudson River steamboats made it clear, the Harlem's owners reasoned, that they would do best by staying inland, well clear of the Hudson River's east shore communities, which were being admirably served by steamboats as they had been since Fulton's successful trial in 1807. In point of fact, the railroad had failed to take adequate account of the disastrous impact the ice-choked Hudson River had upon winter commerce in places like Poughkeepsie. But the distressed merchants of that community didn't: In 1846 they organized a competing venture, the Hudson River Railroad, and with the assistance of the brilliant surveyor and engineer, John Jervis, Jr., laid a route along the east bank of the Hudson that was essentially level for its entire 144-mile length. It was completed in the remarkably brief period of five years. By accomplishing this, the Hudson River Railroad roundly beat out its older, inland competitor, the Harlem, whose route was longer, more labored, and failed to extend to Albany until almost a year after the Hudson's. As a result of

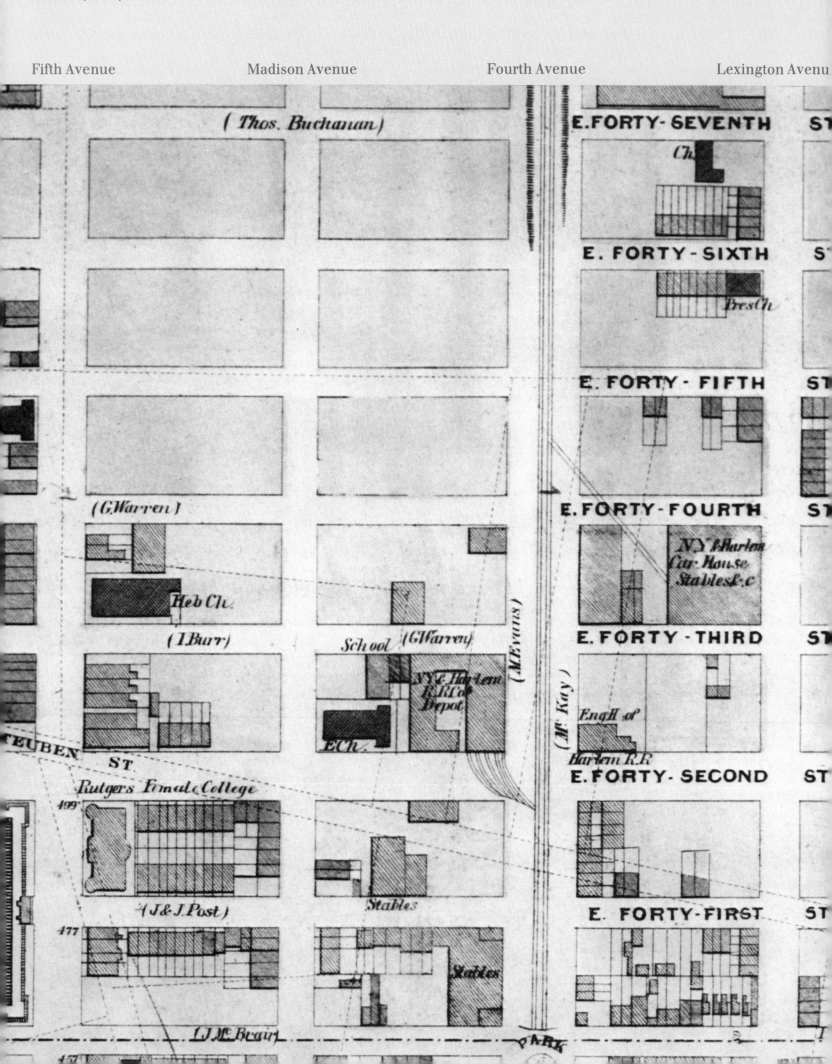

Fourth Avenue is shown continuing northward across 42nd Street, but many blocks remain devoid of any develop- ment in this 1868 land- map from *The Plan of New York City*, Mathew Dripps, publisher.

Fifth Avenue   Madison Avenue   Fourth Avenue   Lexington Avenu

(Thos. Buchanan)

E. FORTY-SEVENTH   ST

Ch

E. FORTY-SIXTH   ST

Pres Ch

E. FORTY-FIFTH   ST

E. FORTY-FOURTH   ST

(G.Warren)

N.Y. Harlem Car House Stables &c

Heb Ch.

E. FORTY-THIRD   ST

(I. Burr)

School (G.Warren)

(M.Evans)

N.Y. Harlem R.R Co's Depot

(Mc Kay)

Eng.H of

E Ch.

Harlem R.R

STEUBEN   ST

E. FORTY-SECOND   ST

Rutgers Female College

499

(J & J. Post)

Stables

E. FORTY-FIRST   ST

477

Stables

(J. McBrair)

PARK

457

its misjudgment, the Harlem was thereafter largely relegated to local service as far as its upstate connections were concerned. Beginning in 1851, long-distance passengers and freight destined northward used the Hudson's superior advantages.

□ Closer to New York, however, the Harlem served other purposes very well. Its Park Avenue route across the Harlem River into Westchester County opened up sections of Manhattan's upper east side, the Bronx, and Westchester to real estate development. And its Woodlawn trackage in today's north Bronx provided an opportunity for another railroad to gain access to Manhattan's traffic, the New York & New Haven. In 1848, after failing to obtain its own rights into New York City, the New Haven successfully negotiated an arrangement to use the Harlem's track, stations, and facilities in order to open rail connections between New Haven and New York.[12] Eventually these would encompass the rest of New England when the railroad later evolved into the gargantuan New York, New Haven & Hartford.

□ As the Harlem, and its new tenant the New Haven, plied their trackage along Manhattan's east side, the Hudson River Railroad entered the city on the west, down the banks of the Hudson past Riverdale, across Spuyten Duyvil, and into two terminals, the first in the west 30s and another, built shortly afterward, at Chambers Street and West Broadway. As the Hudson River Railroad was able to serve the needs of merchants in Poughkeepsie and the other east bank communities to the north, it also provided a main line connection to the Hudson's shoreline in New York City as well. In earlier years the city's shipping had been relegated to the East River, a calmer, narrower waterway protected from the drift of upstate ice floes and convenient to long-distance shipping to New England and Europe. With the increase in the size of ocean-going vessels by the mid-nineteenth century, the Hudson became a more dependable channel than the East River.

□ The barge traffic across and down the Hudson was increasing, too. It was easy to transfer freight from the Hudson's wide array of shipping to the trackage of the adjacent Hudson River Railroad, and the west side of Manhattan below 72nd Street would soon experience commercial and industrial development as a result. The Hudson's freight-handling convenience was clearly superior to that of the east side railroads – whose tracks never approached any harborside connections – but the Hudson's passenger terminals were vastly inferior, particularly their location, lying far from the heart of population along Manhattan's center line and lacking any ease of connection to the Harlem's or New Haven's stations.

□ As New York passed the middle of the 1840s, the Harlem's Madison Square facilities at 26th-27th streets and Fourth Avenue became surrounded with new residential settlements. In 1848 the *Evening Post* said that this part of the city "is rapidly filling up with private dwellings, in many places entire blocks are going up, and in a few years this will be one of the most thickly settled parts of the city. The business of the Harlem Road has made this place what it is. . . ."[13] Obviously the Harlem's owners were aware of the growing viability of its Madison Square station facilities. When a fire in April 1845 destroyed its wood frame depot structure, and when, the next year, the Common Council ordered it to move its steam locomotive facilities still northward to 32nd Street,[14] they did not divest themselves of the site. After dragging their feet for a time, they built a new steam locomotive facility at the northeast corner of 32nd Street and Fourth Avenue in 1847. Shortly thereafter, the Common Council ordered the Harlem to roof over its deep cut down the center of Fourth Avenue from 32nd to 42nd streets, no doubt to limit the dispersal of smoke and noise in the adjacent Murray Hill community. Once again the Common Council had restricted the entry of steam locomotives into the populated section of the city. In 1854, it would act again, and banish the iron horse to the urbanized city's new outer edge, to Fourth Avenue north of 42nd Street, a stipulation that would go into force on January 27, 1856.

□ The Harlem and New Haven invested in a pair of brick passenger stations in 1857; they stood next to one another on the site near Madison Square that had now been identified with railroading in Manhattan for almost a quarter of a century.[15] Here travelers changed from horse-drawn streetcars to larger horse-drawn railroad coaches; the fact that the changeover to steam locomotion lay another fifteen blocks northward was just another inconvenience of operation.

□ The New York & Harlem had failed to achieve its goal as a main route to Albany, but it was doing quite well as a local and commuter line to the suburbs springing up north of the Harlem River. Its revenues were also being significantly increased by the rent it was collecting from New York & New Haven. It was at this point, in 1863, that the brilliant, shrewd, and ruthless enterpriser, "Commodore" Cornelius Vanderbilt, wealthy beyond belief from his steamboat ventures, turned his attention to railroading. In short order he gained control of the Harlem, the Hudson River Railroad, and the New York Central – at that time only a link between Albany and Buffalo. With rail connections that soon ran from New York all the way to Chicago, Vanderbilt merged two of his holdings into the New York Central and Hudson River Railroad, leased the lands of the New York & Harlem, and built a new connecting link between the westerly route of the Hudson line and the easterly one of the Harlem. The trackage of the short-lived Spuyten Duyvil & Port Morris,[16] built on the Bronx side of the Harlem River, made possible Vanderbilt's ingenious rerouting of his rail traffic monopoly that delivered passengers and freight directly into Manhattan without the cumbersome, time-consuming, and costly transfer to ferries or barges to cross the Hudson, required of his competitors.

□ Vanderbilt diverted freight down the west side over the old Hudson River Railroad trackage directly to the Hudson River piers. He shunted his long-distance passengers, via his Spuyten Duyvil connection, over to the east-side route of the Harlem and the New Haven railroads which ran south down Fourth Avenue toward Manhattan's population concentration. This created a collection of trains which badly needed a proper depot to unite all the passengers and equipment and services under one commodious roof. It would have to be a grand, central depot – and that would make a perfect name for it as well.

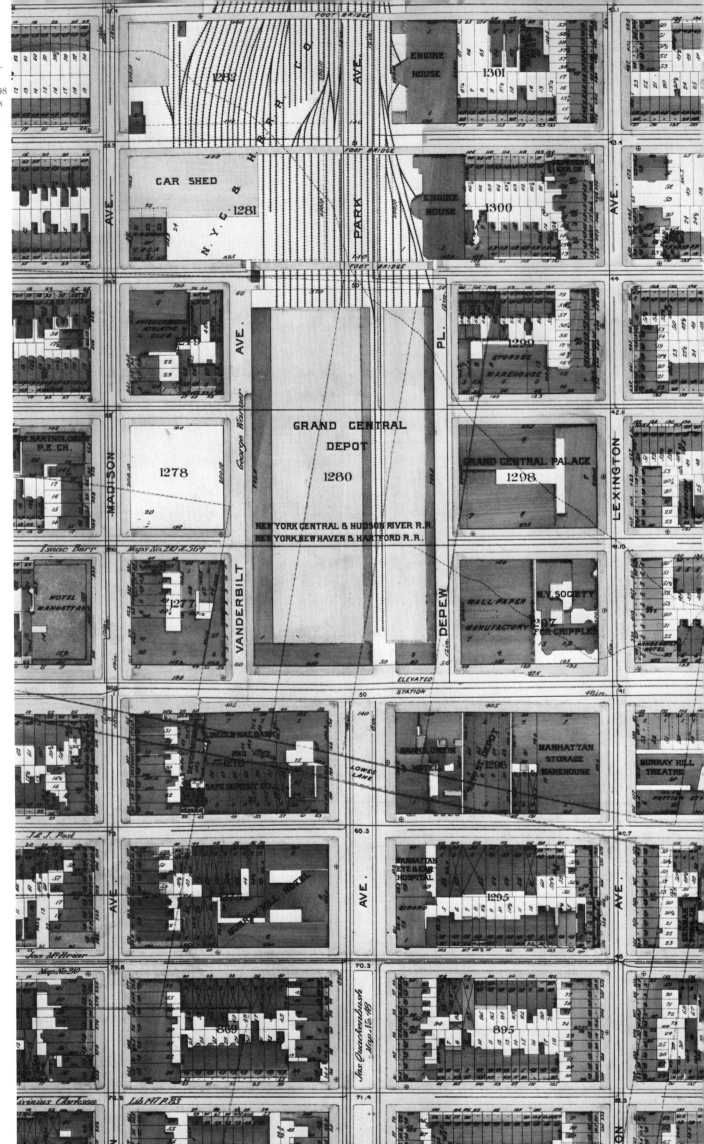

The headhouse of the 1871 Grand Central Depot is the L-shaped structure along Vanderbilt Avenue and 42nd Street shown in this 1898 landmap from *The Atlas of the City of New York*, G. W. Bromley & Company, publisher.

□ Ever since 1857, the locomotive servicing facilities of both the Harlem and New Haven had been located at the intersection of 42nd Street and Fourth Avenue. The Perris Insurance map of 1859 shows the Harlem's blacksmith shop on the southwest corner of the intersection, and a car house and stables, a locomotive house and depot, and cattle sheds along the west side of Fourth Avenue on the three blocks between 42nd and 45th streets. The northeast corner of 42nd Street was the site of the New Haven's locomotive house and a miscellaneous shed. The most abundant land use in the area was empty lots; Madison Avenue would not be opened above 42nd until 1860.

□ There were those who said the 42nd Street site was too far north for the new depot, remote from the city's business center, forty-five long minutes from City Hall via horsecar.[17] But to Vanderbilt, surveying the dense tide of northward growth, the unavailability of land to the south, and the strictures on the use of steam, the site seemed predestined.

□ The 1860s saw more stables, car houses, and a milk depot built by the Harlem added to the existing railroad structures. On the east, however, the waves of immigration were depositing Germans, English, and Irish in the four- and five-story tenements and flats lining Third, Second, and First avenues. Horsecar lines were in full operation down the center of each. By 1860, the city had already reached 59th Street, on the east side at least, and during the Civil War years the side streets started to fill up as well.

□ By the end of the 1860s the immigrants had established some churches, the names of which revealed the mix of their ethnicity – the Swedish Methodist Church on Lexington Avenue and 52nd Street, St. Peter's Lutheran at 46th Street, and St. Agnes Roman Catholic, which still remains, on 43rd Street, west of Third Avenue. Offering social services to the city's new working-class and middle-class residents were a number of institutions that had recently gravitated to the area. Closest to the railroad was the Hospital of the Society for the Relief of the Ruptured and Crippled, built in 1867 on the site of today's Grand Hyatt Hotel. To the south was the Manhattan Eye and Ear Hospital, opened in 1869. And along Lexington were Woman's Hospital and the Episcopal Orphan Home and Asylum.

□ Further to the east, interspersed among the flats, were at least a dozen breweries with names such as Gillig's, Ahle's, Neidlinger Schmidt & Company, and the H. Clausen Steam Brewery. And even farther away from Fourth, hugging the banks of the East River, were a group of slaughter houses to which cattle were driven in the early 1860s across 42nd Street from the Hudson River docks. On the rocks at 42nd Street's east end, the site today of the Tudor City complex, lay Dutch Hill, a poverty-stricken, gang-ridden squatters' community of wooden shacks, goats, and squalor, repeatedly visited by agitated representatives of the city's charity groups trying to render assistance.

□ To the west of the proposed terminal site, the scene was quite different. There lay Fifth Avenue, the city's premier residential street. The battered walls of the Croton Reservoir, upon whose elevated walkway fashionable couples promenaded on Sunday, and the crenellated House of Mansions, designed by Andrew Jackson Davis, across the way, marked Fifth Avenue's intersection with 42nd Street, across which real estate agents once believed fine development would not pass. The destruction, during the Civil War's draft riots, of the Colored Orphan Asylum at Fifth Avenue above 43rd Street helped dispel such concerns. By the end of the 1860s, fine houses of worship had been built along nearby upper Fifth Avenue north of 42nd Street, churches that did not bear the

The air rights development sites north of Grand Central (incorrectly labeled "Station" here) and the Grand Central Terminal Office Building stretching north to 45th Street are evident in this 1916 landmap from *The Atlas of the Borough of Manhattan*, G. W. Bromley & Company, publisher.

ethnic allusions of those to the east. Rather, they continued the social traditions of the churches on Madison and Fifth avenues in the upper 30s, Zion Protestant Episcopal and Brick Presbyterian, and of the charming Chapel of the Holy Trinity at the northeast corner of Madison and 42nd. In 1869 the Episcopal Church of the Heavenly Rest opened on Fifth Avenue above 46th Street, and the noted church architect Leopold Eidlitz gave the city's Reform Jews a splendid Moorish edifice on Fifth Avenue at 43rd in 1868, Temple Emanu-El.

□ Both Fifth and Madison avenues between 34th and 42nd streets were lined with the homes of the wealthy. There, since the middle of the nineteenth century, families bearing such names as Phelps, Dodge, Pyne, Goelet, and Havemayer had resided in refined brownstone townhouses and rowhouses. Following the Civil War, the so-called Flash Age of realty speculation deposited a great many substantial houses above 32nd Street between Fifth and Lexington avenues. In April 1896 a plot of land between Madison and Fifth was turned over four times in just sixty days, at $40,000 the first time, and at $55,000 the fourth.[18] In the midst of this speculation, the Commodore's son, William H. Vanderbilt, who would inherit his father's new interest – vocational and monetary – in railroading, bought the site at the southeast corner of Fifth Avenue and 40th Street. On it he shortly built the Vanderbilt family's first Fifth Avenue residence.[19]

□ With a land boom proclaiming the desirability of the depot's southerly and westerly environs, a family interest already established in that nearby community, and every indication that the area's fashionable families would either continue to reside there or move northward along Fifth and Madison avenues, parallel to the proposed depot's west flank, the Vanderbilts must certainly have been concerned about the impact their new railroad facility would have upon its surroundings – and their neighbors.

□ The plan of the Grand Central Depot of 1871 reflects such a concern. Built across what had been Fourth Avenue, now closed for the depot's construction by an act of the legislature,[20] the structure consisted of an immense utilitarian train shed for railroad cars and a lavish edifice, a "headhouse" in the argot of railroading, for passengers and their baggage. The headhouse was an "L" in plan, its short leg extending along 42nd Street and its long leg running three blocks north along Vanderbilt Avenue, the new addition to the street grid that was supposed to compensate for the interruption of Fourth Avenue.[21] The architectural forms of the headhouse, with their bulbous mansard roofs, did not echo those of European railroad depots – as the great arched train shed it wrapped around did – but rather those of the preeminent palace of Paris, the Louvre. Evidently, one historian has suggested, "the Commodore as an empire builder, was undoubtedly vain enough to feel that there was nothing incongruous in transplanting a palace to serve as his personal headquarters."[22] The "palace," however, served at least one other function: It concealed the 652-foot-long, 200-foot-wide, 100-foot-high semicircular train shed not only from the immediate visibility of adjacent 42nd Street and Vanderbilt Avenue, but also from the Murray Hill community to the south, and from Madi-

son and Fifth avenues to the west. (Empty lots were still for sale along the latter in the early 1870s.) The 1871 depot's lavish facades of brick and cast iron acted to integrate its architecture into the fashionable residential communities that were its neighbors.

□ To the east, however, where the neighborhoods were inhabited by tenements, hospitals, and breweries, at best, the great shed remained clearly visible. Vanderbilt saw no need to conceal his shed from those who were clearly less genteel than the depot's upper-class neighbors.

□ The layout of the L-shaped headhouse, while superficially resembling the plan of the depot's Parisian predecessor, the second Gare du Nord (1861–1865),[23] achieved its special role in shaping the form of Manhattan the hard way. In this first Grand Central, as in its Paris counterpart, passengers boarding trains all departed from the *west* leg of the depot; they embarked from one of the three sets of adjacent waiting rooms and ticket offices, one for each of the railroads using the terminal. But as each departing train left the depot, it had to cross over to the *east* side of the tracks to make its way north out of Manhattan. Not so in Paris, where French railroads then – as now – run opposite hand, using the British system.

□ Similarly, incoming trains were also required to cross over, because Grand Central's incoming arrival area was on the *east* side of the 42nd Street leg, opposite the entrance to the Park Avenue underpass below Murray Hill. The crossover of incoming and outgoing trains, to permit what is called "left-handed running," continued until the new Grand Central Terminal opened in 1913.[24]

□ This awkward crossover maneuver, involving 130 train movements daily in 1871,[25] was a stiff price to pay for Vanderbilt's desire to respond to the needs of the adjacent community, but it enabled Manhattan to develop along Fifth Avenue and environs while injecting the workings of a major railroad terminal into what would one day become its very heart.

□ Vanderbilt may have effectively camouflaged his depot from the eyes of affluent New Yorkers through the careful placement of his headhouse, but other characteristics of steam-powered passenger railroads were not as easy to disguise. Locomotives had to be turned around for their return journey, they needed coal and water to generate steam, and they required prodigious amounts of lubrication to overcome friction. Since three railroads used the depot, three separate sets of turntables and servicing facilities were developed, all on the Lexington Avenue side, of course, where the chugging and hissing and the smoke and cinders couldn't offend people of quality.

□ The passengers in the train shed were insulated from the visible environmental problems associated with steam locomotion by a system called the "flying switch," whereby an incoming locomotive would disengage from its train and speed up and out of its way before the train entered the shed, to be slowed and stopped by the skill of brakemen; outgoing engines would back in only at the very last moment before coupling to their trains. But once trains left the shed, all of these fancy stratagems were left behind. The railroads' street-level route up the Fourth Avenue right-of-way was an environmental disaster. No wonder the block-long Schaeffer brewery established its socially offensive premises between 50th and 51st streets, and William Steinway built his piano factory be-

Following World War II, air rights sites were developed for the second time. The Pan Am Building (1963), which replaced the Grand Central Terminal Building behind the terminal itself, appears on this 1955 landmap, updated to 1966, from the *Manhattan Land Book*, G. W. Bromley & Company, publisher.

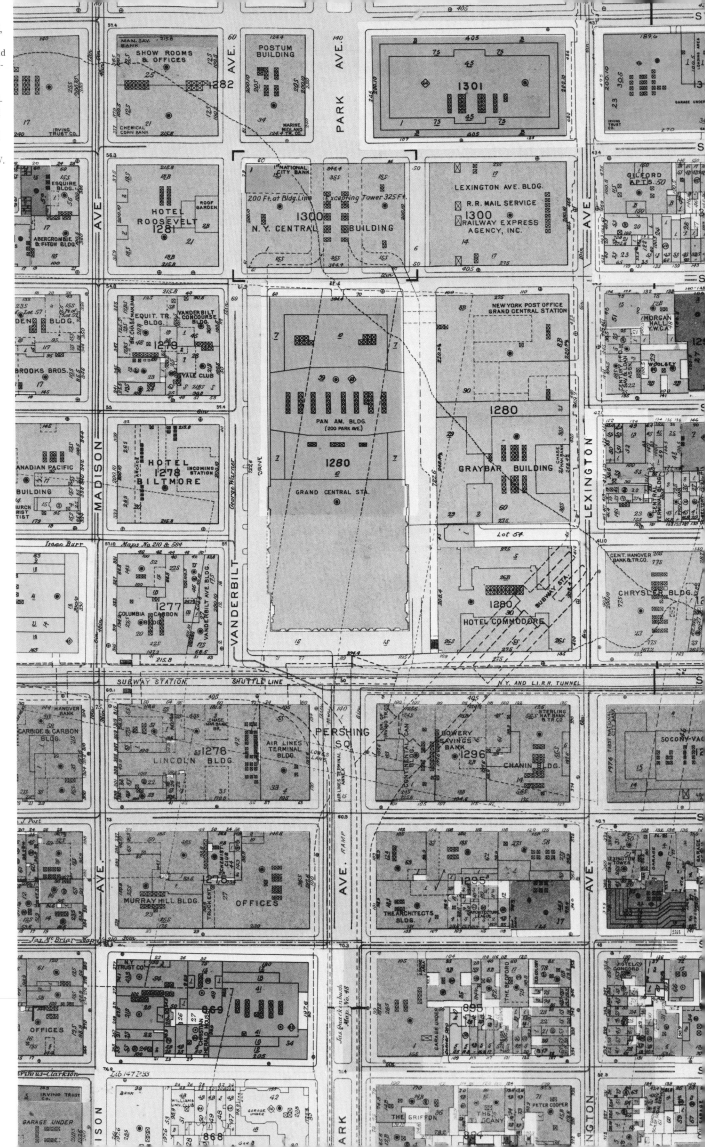

tween 52nd and 53rd streets. Though the railroads' tracks, by now four in number, were by 1875 lowered into a partly covered cut which began at 49th Street,[26] the smoke from the trains continued to depress potential development along Park Avenue, particularly near the fan of tracks just north of the shed, between 45th and 49th streets.

□ On the depot's other sides, along 42nd Street, and on nearby Lexington, Park, and Vanderbilt, its impact was being felt in other ways, but slowly. For at least seven years after the depot opened, goats were still being raised on the northeast corner of 42nd at Lexington: "They gamboled on the stoop of the Hospital for the Ruptured and the Crippled,"[27] across Lexington. Between the hospital and the depot, the Croton Market was in full swing, purveying produce to passengers and local folk from 1869 until the late 1880s, when the Annex to Grand Central was built on its site.

□ How, then, did the depot affect its surroundings?

□ Long-distance travelers sought a variety of facilities—shelter, a hot bath, or a meal for those arriving; last-minute necessities, a snack, some tobacco, an item of toiletry for those departing.[28] Naturally enough, the new depot drew hotels, eateries, and a miscellany of small shops to its vicinity.[29] With the city's fashionable hotel district then still a mile away to the south, a number of small, unpretentious hotels sprang up at Park and 42nd. On the southeast corner was the Reunion – its name reflecting a frequently observed event around the depot. (It was soon renamed the Westchester.) Next door, on the 42nd Street side, came Riggs House; on the Park Avenue frontage, in 1874 the Grand Union Hotel appeared, absorbing the other two hotels and thereby validating its name. The Grand Union's roof sported mansard towers of ogee curvature, relating its architecture to that of Grand Central's across the way. Its "gay blade" owner averred that a successful hotel must offer "hair curlers, hot house roses, and hand painted pianos";[30] clearly, even with the appearance of the Grand Union, the city's fashionable hotels continued to lie a mile away.

□ On the southwest corner of Park and 42nd, there sprang up a bunch of saloons and restaurants and an all-night food stand, the Park Avenue Oyster House.[31] Galway's Grocery, Mrs. Gibson's Candy Store, and Frank Schoonmaker's drugstore and tobacco shop were among the other retail merchants attracted to the area.[32] "The street was composed of the most modest homes, rude clapboard shacks fronted the

Cooper Square, New-York.

8092. GRAND CENTRAL STATION, NEW YORK.

COPYRIGHT, 1905, BY DETROIT PUBLISHING CO.

Fifth Avenue and Waldorf Astoria Hotel, New York.

12138 FIFTH AVENUE AND 42ND. STREET, NEW YORK

COPR. DETROIT PUBLISHING CO.

6286. FIFTH AVENUE, NEW YORK.

COPYRIGHT, 1902, BY DETROIT PHOTOGRAPHIC CO.

railroad station, and in the shacks cheap meals were served; there were some barrooms and a very inconspicuous hotel was on the corner," remembered one businessman when polled in 1921 about his recollections of a half century earlier.[33] By 1875 Charles & Company, until recently purveyors of specialty foods for travelers, had moved from the old Harlem/New Haven station at Madison Square to 43rd Street just off Vanderbilt, away from the bustling 42nd Street thoroughfare, where they would serve Grand Central Depot's users. More common in the area, however, was the phenomenon of the huge, blank-walled fireproof storage warehouse. The Manhattan Storage Warehouse and the Lincoln Safe Deposit and Storage Warehouse were the largest.

◻ Of all the changes the 1871 depot wrought, the most important was that it attracted other transit modes to its location, means of connecting the terminal with those parts of town that neither the railroads nor their commuter routes served. In the years immediately following the depot's opening, not one omnibus line served the station. Perhaps the critics had been correct: The depot *was* too far uptown. (Omnibuses charged 10 cents per ride, twice the fare of the horsecar, and they didn't run after midnight or on Sundays.)[34]

◻ Though omnibuses did eventually establish connections to Grand Central, the primary access to it that first decade was via the horsecar lines. For only a nickel one could take a car along Second, Third, or Fourth avenues, with the Fourth Avenue cars using the old Murray Hill "tunnel" and passing right in front of the depot before continuing their journey north on Madison. The Lexington Avenue horsecar actually terminated at Grand Central: "Passengers will find it more rapid and pleasant than by the Fourth Avenue line," proclaimed an 1873 guidebook.[35]

◻ By the end of the 1870s, however, public transportation in New York was to be revolutionized by the introduction of elevated rapid transit. Latticed iron structures were advancing up Second, Third, Sixth, and Ninth avenues. On their tracks belched steam engines pulling wooden coaches filled with people to pseudo-Swiss chalet stations balanced precariously above the streets. The Third Avenue elevated, first operated on August 26, 1878, ran to Grand Central's very doorstep via a spur that stretched west along 42nd Street from the el's main line. But direct connection was brief; by September, the Third Avenue line had bypassed its 42nd Street spur, leaving behind a two-block shuttle connection whose elevated viaduct and station were not removed until 1923.[36]

◻ The four Manhattan elevateds speeded travel high above the congestion of the city's streets; their long fingers opened up new areas of the city, a city whose official limits already had been enlarged by the annexation of today's western Bronx in 1874. By 1883 the City of Brooklyn across the river was linked to New York by Roebling's great bridge, and by the end of the 1880s three elevated lines would be in operation there, with ferry connections to Manhattan. By the turn of the century, elevateds would be running over the suburban line into the Bronx, and New York would be Greater New York, a metropolis of 3.4 million people, encompassing five boroughs and over 300 square miles.

◻ As the city moved toward the twentieth century, traffic through and around Grand Central grew apace. In 1884 a truly splendid hostelry, the Murray Hill Hotel, came to Park Avenue's west side between 40th and 41st streets, and other small but respectable hotels appeared on 42nd Street – like the Wellington, a former townhouse, at the northwest corner of Madison. Across the avenue was the new Holy Trinity, which replaced the earlier country chapel in 1874 and was soon labeled "The Church of the Holy Oilcloth" after its unusual polychromy. Two blocks north and across Madison Avenue stood St. Bartholomew's, completed in 1876, a ponderous design characterized by a newspaper in 1889 as "neither imposing nor attractive."[37] It didn't matter; it was ". . . the Vanderbilts' church, known in clubdom as the shrine of silk stockings . . ." where ". . . W. H. Vanderbilt prayed and passed the golden plate, but never without laying on it the heaviest coin of all . . . "[38] The expectation that society would cross 42nd Street had come to pass, and the Vanderbilts crossed with the rest, despite the propinquity of their mock-Louvre depot only a block to the east.

◻ Momentum once achieved is difficult to contain. By 1896 the little four-story Wellington Hotel had been demolished and the spectacular – and far larger – Manhattan Hotel had taken its place, along with the places of the adjoining brownstones along Madison. The same year saw Holy Trinity, barely two decades old, demolished as well. It was clear that the great number of passengers and trains that Grand Central was handling by the 1890s demanded an expansion of its facilities. Between 1898 and 1900, the depot's three stories became six, the Louvre-like mansards evolved into neo-Baroque cupolas, and the facility's name briefly became Grand Central Station.[39] By now the depot was handling three times the number of trains that it did at its opening in 1871.[40] The century was turning, and minor adjustments could no longer respond to the explosive growth of the city and the passenger traffic that was drawn to it.

◻ Outside the station, horsecar lines had been converted into cable cars beginning in 1885,[41] following San Francisco's pattern. And even as New Yorkers had begun to adjust to this new transportation improvement, yet another was introduced: electric motive power. Using those same slots down the middle of their tracks, streetcars could now pick up an electric current that made them run more efficiently than ever. Clearly, "clean" electric power was proving itself as dependable as steam and environmentally much more desirable. By the turn of the century even the elevateds placed their dinky steam engines in storage and adopted electricity.[42]

◻ It took a tragic accident in the tunnel under Park Avenue to persuade the railroads entering Grand Central that electricity would be their answer as well. On the morning of January 8, 1902, with visibility diminished because of smoke and plumes of water vapor condensing in the cold winter air, a New York Central train ran a red signal and plowed into a stopped New Haven train ahead of it, killing fifteen persons outright.[43] Only one year elapsed before the legislature placed a ban on steam locomotives using the Park Avenue tunnel and gave the railroad the authority to build the station into the immense two-level electrified terminal we know today.[44]

FOUR TRACK SUBWAY AT SPRING STREET   NEW YORK.

TWENTY-THIRD STREET
SUBWAY STATION, NEW YORK.

Aunt Hannah died Wednesday night
funeral Friday morning am going M.B.

2050 Metropolitan Building,
New York.

Union Square looking North, New York, N.Y.

25908

Union Square, New York.

□ The plan to electrify the railroads entering Grand Central, enabling them to be placed deep below the street surface, was not lost upon those who found fault with the clattering elevateds and the noisy, gloomy, cluttered streets that lay beneath their lattice work. Why not *underground* rapid transit, a subway, that would move passengers beneath the streets using the newly proven technology of electricity? In 1904, the Interborough Rapid Transit Company, the IRT, accomplished just that. The city's first subway line ran north from the Manhattan end of the Brooklyn Bridge, at City Hall, to 42nd Street, then jogged west to Times Square, and turned north again, up Broadway, to open the sluggish upper west side to dense residential development.

□ To get through Manhattan's pregrid jumble of streets, the IRT's planners followed a strategy similar to that used by the New York & Harlem back in the 1830s. Lower Broadway was simply too congested to be considered. They chose the straightest and widest thoroughfare available, not the Bowery – now encumbered by the Third Avenue el – but Lafayette Street, which had been cut through since the 1830s. Once the four tracks snaked their way to Union Square, they followed the same pathfinding route of the Harlem Railroad up Fourth and Park avenues, almost predictably into the lap of Grand Central, just before which they made their turn to the west, cutting across the plot of land on the southwest corner of 42nd Street and Park Avenue. Here, in 1906, the IRT's August Belmont would add another fine hotel, the twenty-two-story Belmont, the tallest building on 42nd Street at that time.

□ Just as the elevateds had for two decades made outer parts of the city rapidly accessible and therefore ripe for development, the subway did the same for the inner city, particularly the part between Union Square and Grand Central. The IRT's stops, conveniently placed at 18th, 23rd, and 28th streets, gave Fourth Avenue – today's Park Avenue South – greater accessibility. The Metropolitan Life Insurance Company had already shown the way through its spectacular office building complex at 23rd, which included five office buildings constructed since 1890. Drawn by this appealing situation, developers built block after block of loft structures, to which textile and print companies gravitated from lower Manhattan. Beginning in 1905, Fourth Avenue's parallel walls of additional loft buildings above 17th Street would increasingly frame the Beaux-Arts facade of the new Grand Central Terminal under construction at the apex of its axis. Like City Hall did a century earlier, Grand Central Terminal would face "the city to the south," both buildings relegating their rear facades toward uptown. Grand Central's rear took the form of a "bustle" (called the Grand Central Terminal *Building*), an agglomeration of anonymous back-office space that spanned the behind-the-scenes baggage-handling activities.

□ The new terminal, which would open on February 2, 1913,[45] had expanded its coverage of Manhattan's real estate from twenty-three acres in 1900 to almost forty-eight acres,[46] encompassing some thirty city blocks. The additional acreage, having been artificially depressed in value, was purchased at bargain prices. While its waiting rooms, the grandiose concourse, and its arched windows and vaulted ceilings called out Welcome to passengers, its sprawling acreage devoted to yards and trackage, now smoke-free, called out Opportunity to developers.

□ The cost of electrification had not come cheaply. The veritable Mesabi Range of construction operations that carved the double level of tracks from Manhattan's unyielding schist was also costly. William J. Wilgus, the railroad's chief engineer, in planning this vast enterprise, recognized the magnitude of these costs and proposed that the space above these yards, once they had been completed – the air rights – be sold to developers. The income the railroad would realize from the sale of these rights would compensate it for its capital outlay for electrification and construction.

□ In a January 25, 1913 issue of *Harper's Weekly*, six years after Wilgus had left the railroad, there appeared an ad for The Terminal City, a development over the New York Central's yards. The ad prophesied that the complex would be "the greatest civic development ever undertaken." "It will embrace hotels and modern apartment houses," it went on,

Hotel Manhattan, N. Y. City.

PERSHING SQ. BUILDING, NEW YORK CITY

HOTEL COMMODORE, NEW YORK CITY.

GRAND CENTRAL PALACE, NEW YORK CITY.

PARK-LEXINGTON BUILDING AND GRAND CENTRAL DEPOT, NEW YORK CITY.

"convention and exhibition halls, clubs and restaurants, and department stores and speciality shops." The image conveyed by the ad and the publicity that accompanied it showed a development of buildings lining Park Avenue that was as neatly trimmed as a topiary garden.

□ While development came as predicted, the neatness of the Beaux-Arts designs depicted in the ad did not. Speculation was too great a force. Builders made their deals with the railroad as best and as quickly as they could. Nevertheless, despite different architects, building types, and configurations of height and plan, a unity of appearance did emerge, partly because of the common note of a limestone base used for most of the structures, and the then-fashionable neo-Classical vocabulary.

□ In the years between the terminal's opening and America's entry into World War I, the Biltmore Hotel, the Yale Club, and two sizable office buildings were completed on the railroad's property across Vanderbilt Avenue from the terminal. The years of developmental dormancy for the terminal's air-rights area were ending at the same time that the commercialization of nearby Fifth and Madison avenues was beginning. Real estate magnate Robert W. Goelet completed the Ritz-Carlton Hotel on Madison's west side between 46th and 47th streets in 1910, and its success was legion – despite the fact that for years its windows looked out over the still-uncovered rail yards.[47] Brooks Brothers and Abercrombie and Fitch were established south of the Ritz by 1917.[48]

□ Along lower Park Avenue, south of the terminal, the agreement known as the Murray Hill Convenant (of 1847) and the zeal of Murray Hill's old families, who went to court early and often to enforce it and thereby protect the area against commercial encroachment, kept this part of the avenue residential, as it remains today.[49] By 1912 a group of architects built a multistory cooperative loft building, 101 Park Avenue, for their coprofessionals' office needs. This helped call attention to the office building opportunities of 42nd Street in front of Grand Central.

□ As the original IRT route had been drawn to and past Grand Central in 1904, other transportation modes were attracted in the decade the new terminal was under construction. The 1902 plan to connect the IRT to the New York Central's suburban level tracks was never realized,[50] nor was the dream to extend the Hudson and Manhattan line – today's PATH system – from the terminal it reached in 1909 at 33rd Street to a new terminal under the IRT tracks in front of Grand Central.[51] An architect even proposed a meandering new diagonal avenue to facilitate vehicular movement between the city's two key railroad hubs. (Pennsylvania Station had become, by 1911, Manhattan's other railroad passenger facility.)[52]

□ Of all the proposals made, only two came into being: an underground trolley car connection below the East River to Queens, which became the IRT Flushing Line,[53] and the extension of the east side and west side legs of the original IRT line itself. This latter improvement added a major dimension to Grand Central's role as a transportation nexus. The popular and heretofore overcrowded IRT was converted from its

original Z-shaped configuration to an H-shaped route. The southerly Fourth Avenue leg, on the east side, was extended northward on Lexington Avenue. The northerly Broadway leg, on the west side, was extended southward along Seventh Avenue. And the old east-west jog, along 42nd Street, became today's Shuttle, linking the two now separate north-south routes by becoming the crossbar of the H. This more than doubled the length of the IRT's trackage, not only adding immeasurably to the number of people who passed through the Grand Central area, but also opening two strategic building development sites at street level.

□ The diagonal path that the east side IRT was required to take from Park to Lexington avenues forced the demolition of outmoded structures on two pivotal 42nd Street corners: the old Grand Union Hotel at Park and the old hospital and the adjacent wallpaper factory at Lexington. While the latter two became the site of the Commodore Hotel, completed in 1919 and integrated into the terminal's workings, the Grand Union hotel site became a *cause celebre*. An empty lot during the war years awaiting the completion of subway construction, the site caught the attention of those who wished to see a proper memorial built to commemorate returning veterans of World War I. The proposal was for a convention center to be called Victory Hall, a structure meant to substitute for the outmoded Madison Square Garden which had for many years occupied the former Harlem/New Haven station site at 26th Street. The most persuasive argument its boosters advanced for placing the convention hall opposite Grand Central was, of course, the site's superb accessibility to transit.[54]

□ Victory Hall's proponents failed to secure the site,[55] but their efforts called attention to its commercial advantages. In short order it was privately purchased (at a $3 million price tag), and the Bowery Savings Bank and the twenty-seven-story Pershing Square Building went up in 1923. The latter took its place across the 42nd Street intersection from the twenty-two-story Hotel Belmont, to frame Park Avenue opposite Grand Central.

□ The twenties were boom years for Manhattan real estate. Office space was in demand and accessibility to a work force was crucial. Businesses long identified with downtown were moving north, particularly to the area increasingly referred to as the Grand Central Zone. In September of 1920, the *Times* announced, "One of the outstanding features of the real estate market has been the pronounced buying and leasing movement in the Forty-second Street section, which has resulted in a new banking centre, a 'Little Wall Street.'"[56] So desirable was a midtown location among bankers that the Manhattan Hotel of 1896 on Madison at 42nd Street was converted into the uptown branch offices of National City Bank in 1921.

□ On the Lexington Avenue side of the terminal, only a block away from the Third Avenue elevated's blighting influence, less change was evident. A new Grand Central Palace occupied an air-rights site between 46th and 47th streets, replacing the earlier one to the south that had been removed for the staging of terminal construction. But its attraction was a specialized one, catering largely to only-to-the-trade activities. Two blocks south was a pompous neo-Classical post office, designed to be expanded but left incomplete to this day. People who were attracted to Madison or Fifth avenues rarely used Lexington.

The Barclay
in NEW YORK

The Ambassador, New York City.

72275   WALDORF-ASTORIA HOTEL - - PARK AVENUE, NEW YORK CITY

177   Chrysler, Daily News, Chanin, Lincoln and Lefcourt Buildings, New York City

2A-H119

CHANIN BUILDING - NEW YORK CITY

The Lincoln Building, New York City.

CHRYSLER BUILDING, NEW YORK CITY   50

14844

□ It was to the rear of Grand Central, however, where Terminal City had been postulated, that the real action was taking place. The buildings that were being constructed over the yards on either side of Park Avenue north of 47th Street did not extend the office building explosion that could be found at Grand Central's south and west. Instead, they were monumental and dignified apartment buildings and residential hotels, all with doormen, and many with interior courtyards. In the midst of midtown, this area had become an exclusive residential enclave. A number of factors explain this, but the primary one was that Grand Central itself and the "bustle" that had been built onto its rear – the inauspicious five-story structure with the confusing name, the Grand Central Terminal Building – stemmed the tide of office building development moving toward 42nd Street from the south.

□ The terminal also impeded the natural north-south flow of vehicles and pedestrians at street level between 42nd and 45th streets. To detour via Lexington Avenue meant negotiating a dowdy thoroughfare of cheap shops. To detour via Vanderbilt placed one on a gloomy street almost totally devoid of any shops. (Since its structures lay over tracks below, there could be none of the low-rent cellar storage areas that fashionable stores like those on Madison or Fifth avenues needed.) Furthermore, Vanderbilt was not a through street; it began suddenly on 42nd and ended just as abruptly at 46th. And the perimeter driveway around Grand Central that would eventually carry Park Avenue's traffic took a long time to complete. The viaduct over 42nd Street didn't open until 1919, and only the west half of the drive was available until 1928. Even so, though the viaduct was a short-cut through the area, and therefore a cabbie's dream to this day, it did little for local congestion except to encourage it.

□ Grand Central had become a buffer between upper Park Avenue and the "maelstrom of seething commercialization"[57] to its south. It was in the years that immediately followed the completion of the terminal that a spectacular array of luxury apartment structures and hotels were built over the yards and beyond. The apartments displayed such names as the Marguery, the Park Lane Apartments, and the Montana, with others, just as posh, identified only by addresses: 277 by McKim, Mead and White, 280 and 300 both by Warren and Wetmore. Number 300 Park included a new Sherry's, two stories of restaurant facilities that could be rented or simply called on the house phone to deliver up a meal or a banquet. The hotels included the Barclay, the Chatham, and the Ambassador, which catered to an exclusive clientele, as well as the Roosevelt. (The Waldorf-Astoria, completed in 1931, occupied the last major air-rights property to be developed.)

□ During the early twenties, rental apartments at 300 Park Avenue ranged in price from $5,000 to $50,000 per year.[58] Annual rentals at $30,000 and $40,000 were not uncommon elsewhere, and such apartments were "fully rented and have a waiting list."[59] Park Avenue above Grand Central was hailed in the early 1930s as "the ideal residential locality for the aristocracy and wealth of the city who desired to live conveniently near 'business' (and yet not actually have their homes on a business street) . . . the mere address 'Park Avenue' spells Prestige."[60] Coincidentally, the opening of the terminal in 1913 corresponded with the establishment of the federal income tax, which helped persuade the affluent that town-house living was too extravagant and that apartments, with less need for live-in servants, were just as fashionable but more economical.

□ As the twenties became more frantic with speculation, more and more office space was added along and below 42nd Street, seemingly on smaller and smaller plots. Manhattan Storage Warehouse gave way to the fifty-six-story Chanin Building; Lincoln Storage gave way to the fifty-four-story Lincoln Building; an innocuous five-story business building gave way to the magnificent seventy-seven-story spire of the Chrysler Building. Other skyscrapers rose anonymously from the side streets: 10 East 40th Street (forty-five stories); 22 East 40th Street (forty-five stories); 295 Madison Avenue (forty-five stories). Looking back at the period in 1931, a real estate commentator would write, "Ten years ago [1921] 42nd Street gloried in its four 'towering' skyscrapers . . . beautiful structures [that] were the pride of all Midtown. . . . Today, over 50 new skyscrapers pierce the sky in this pulsating Midtown district, which tower so far above these former spires that they appear like small town buildings."[61]

□ As the twenties were frenetic, the thirties and forties were a period of sadness, war, and recovery. In 1931, despite its elegance and popularity, the Hotel Belmont came down. Its owners had assumed that the stock market crash of '29 was only a temporary setback, and decided that its site alongside the new Lincoln Building, the latter assessed at over $20 million, was simply too valuable to use for a hotel! But the depression only got worse, and the vacant site became a beer garden until the eve of World War II, when the low, Art Moderne Airlines Terminal Building went up to provide bus connection facilities to the nation's newest form of public transportation, the airplane. It did so until traffic congestion in the Grand Central Zone made its services undependable. Now, after three decades the site once again contains a structure – the corporate world headquarters of Philip Morris – sizable enough to balance the Pershing Square Building across the way, thus reinforcing the significance of that gateway site and joining the Grand Hyatt and Harley Hotels recently added in 42nd Street's renaissance of the 1980s.

□ World War II prevented any further development in midtown until 1947, when an office building was completed at 57th Street and Park Avenue. Again, Park Avenue was seeing redevelopment, despite a comment rendered back in 1937 and equally applicable even today: "The fame of Park Avenue is so great that it has generally been forgotten how recent it is."[62] Neither the quality of the architecture, the prestige addresses, nor public opposition stopped developers from removing from Park Avenue's frontages the refined structures that the electrification of Grand Central Terminal had made possible only twenty years earlier. On the contrary, the keys to redevelopment were all available: single owners or lessees, obviating costly and time-consuming negotiations to assemble sites; sufficiently large properties, affording ready development; and–usually–land owned by the railroad, whose particular cooperation would be needed in those cases where the new giants were to be built while trains continued to operate.

171:—GRAND CENTRAL TERMINAL

AND NEW YORK CENTRAL BUILDING, NEW YORK. 40788

NEW YORK CENTRAL BUILDIN . .IEW YORK CITY.

PARK AVENUE, SHOWING MODERN APARTMENT HOUSES, NEW YORK CITY,

12   PARK AVENUE SOUTH FROM 57TH STREET, NEW YORK CITY

□ The result of all this was an almost complete remake of Park Avenue from 46th to 59th streets: In 1957 the Montana Apartments, at twelve stories, became Seagram's House, at forty stories. In 1960, the Marguery, at twelve stories, became Union Carbide, at fifty-two. In 1964, the apartments at 277 Park, at twelve stories, became Chemical Bank, at fifty stories. And so on, until the fashionable residential enclave in the heart of midtown's business district itself became midtown's fashionable business district. The only significant remnant of the pre-1930 era was the New York Central's own office building, dating from 1929, which spanned Park Avenue between 46th and 45th streets and contained the portals to the circumferential drive around the terminal. Its distinctive silhouette gave Park Avenue what little composure remained. That composure was not to last for long.

□ Grand Central's busiest year was 1947, but its value as a transportation hub began to wane after World War II and the railroads began to seek other sources of income from its site. The first clear indication of trouble was the appearance, in the main concourse, of the giant Kodak transparency in 1950. By 1954, a plan had been unveiled to demolish the entire terminal plus its backdoor bustle, to build Grand Central City, a 6-million-square-foot development.[63] While it did not materialize, the Pan Am Building did, and by 1963 that fifty-nine-story office building emerged from the site of the six-story Grand Central Terminal Building to conceal the old New York Central Building's silhouette from lower Park Avenue and camouflage it from upper Park. On the other hand, through its escalator connections with the terminal's main concourse, Pan Am removed the once impenetrable barrier to street-level public movement through the complex. Finally Grand Central had become part of an effective north-south pedestrian link.

□ With Pan Am completed, the New York Central in 1968 turned to other pursuits. It merged with the Pennsylvania Railroad to form the Penn Central, and entertained a proposal for a fifty-five-story tower over the main terminal building itself, to be designed by Marcel Breuer and Associates. When this project failed to obtain the approval of the city's Landmarks Preservation Commission, yet another tower was commissioned, this time one that obliterated the exterior of the terminal entirely while rehabilitating its main concourse.[64]

□ Despite these threats, Grand Central Terminal remains a vital node in midtown's dynamics as well as a memorial to its own crucial role in the shaping and the reshaping of midtown, the city's second business district. Built across Park Avenue long before it bore that name, Grand Central's fortunes have in many ways been linked to that thoroughfare:

In all of the newest New York – the golden city of a million jewels and ten thousand lofty towers – there is nothing else so fascinating, so bewildering, so economic, so beautiful as the recent structural developments in Park Avenue just north of the huge new Grand Central Terminal. The black-breasted and grime-producing railroad yard that formerly stood there has disappeared. Electricity, the most recent and most efficient handmaiden of transportation, has given back to a great city that which years ago was taken from it – its heart.[65]

□ This excerpt from a commercial house organ in 1921 is dated, yet in many ways it still marvelously serves to sum up the era when Grand Central was shaper to the city, a vital gateway to a burgeoning metropolis. Its role as a living catalyst, felicitously gathering together the myriad activities of Manhattan's heart, is yet to be fully realized.

1. **Laws of the State of New York**, 1832, Chapter 101; ibid., 1833, Chapter 309.
2. Charles King, **Progress of the City of New York During the Last Fifty Years** (New York, 1852), p.62.
3. **New York Herald**, 3 September 1803, in Isaac Newton Phelps Stokes, **The Iconography of Manhattan Island**, 6 vols.(New York, 1915-1928), chronology, vol. 5 (hereafter cited as INPS).
4. Clarence Hornung, **Wheels Across America** (New Brunswick, 1959), p. 34.
5. **New York Gazette & General Advertiser**, 5 August 1834, as cited in INPS.
6. The first omnibuses accommodated 12 passengers each, attained a speed of 5 miles per hour, and charged fares ranging between 12 and 35 cents, depending upon distances covered.
7. **New York Herald**, 8 October 1864, as quoted in Harry James Carman, **The Street Surface Railway Franchises of New York City** (New York, 1919), pp. 29, 30 n.
8. Horsecars accommodated 40 passengers each, attained a speed of 12 miles per hour, and charged a fare of 25 cents, which was rapidly reduced as their popularity and numbers increased. Historian Benson J. Lossing, in 1884, observed that for 25 years after their introduction, streetcars were a unique New York City phenomenon.
9. In the report accompanying the Commissioners Plan of 1811, an optimism was already evident regarding the early development of Haerlem, as they spelled it: "It is not improbable that considerable numbers may be collected at Haerlem, before the high hills to the southward of it shall be built upon as a City . . . ." A number of the New York & Harlem's incorporators were listed as subscribers to the published report and no doubt were encouraged to buy land in Harlem by the report's predictions.
10. The earliest successful trial of a steam locomotive, one invented by George Stephenson, took place in England in 1814. The first public passenger railroad in the world, also using steam locomotives developed by Stephenson, occurred on the Stockton & Darlington railway in 1825.
11. An 1832 amendment to the New York & Harlem's original charter prohibited propulsion other than by horsepower south of 14th Street. A boiler explosion in 1835 delayed permanent introduction of steam locomotives until the connection to Harlem was completed. By then the railroad had decided that this site was a convenient one for servicing both means of motive power, steam and horse. Only rarely would steam locomotives venture southward, as on July 4, 1839, when they were called south by lack of sufficient horses to accommodate the celebrating crowds. An ensuing boiler explosion at Union Square, which killed five and injured some 16 others, served to lay the groundwork to restrict steam propulsion's terminus even more severely.
12. According to Carl W. Condit in **The Port of New York**, 2 vols., (Chicago, 1980), vol. 1, p. 30, "the generous agreement extended by the New York [and Harlem] road was regarded by the New Haven officers as guaranteeing a right of entry, a joint use of properties, and all rights of tenancy, these in turn carrying with them a right of perpetual easement over the Harlem lines. The arrangements led the New Haven directors to regard themselves as virtual co-owners of the lessee's stations and to believe that they were entitled not only to consultation over all matters of operation and construction, but also to share in the numerous real estate and air-rights ventures of the Harlem and its successors."
13. **Evening Post**, 12 November 1847.
14. **Resolutions Approved by Mayor**, XII:216. Ibid., XIII:377.
15. William D. Middleton, **Grand Central** (San Marino, California, 1977), p. 15. Carroll L.V. Meeks, **The Railroad Station** (New Haven, 1956), p. 73.
16. Middleton, **Grand Central**, p. 23.
17. Ibid.
18. Arthur Pond, **The Golden Earth** (New York, 1935), pp. 133, 134.
19. Henry Collins Brown, **Fifth Avenue Old and New, 1824–1924** (New York, 1924), p. 83.
20. **Laws of the State of New York**, 1869, Chapter 919.
21. Ibid.
22. Meeks, **The Railroad Station**, pp. 100, 101.
23. Ibid., fig. 49.
24. Middleton, **Grand Central**, pp. 29, 30.
25. Ibid.
26. Condit, **Port of New York**, vol. 1, p. 93.
27. Letter from V.P. Gibney in Frank Schoonmaker, **Yesterday and Today on Forty-second Street** (New York, 1922), p. 41.
28. In addition to long-distance passengers, the depot also served a sizable number of commuters to stations north of the Harlem River, in today's Bronx and Westchester, as well as to stations at 60th, 73rd, 86th, 110th, and 126th streets.
29. Schoonmaker, **Yesterday and Today**, pp. 38, 44, 45.
30. Leslie Dorsey and Janice Devine, **Fare Thee Well** (New York, 1964), p. 89.
31. Ibid., p. 17.
32. Ibid., pp. 44, 45.
33. Letter from Charles Elliot Warren in Schoonmaker, **Yesterday and Today**, pp. 42, 43.
34. Wood's **Illustrated Hand-Book to New York** (New York, 1873), p.126.
35. Ibid., p. 74.
36. Joseph Cunningham and Leonard O. DeHart, **A History of the New York City Subway System, Part I: The Manhattan Els and the I.R.T.** (New York, 1976), pp. 9, 60.
37. **The [New York] Sun**, 3 February 1889.
38. Ibid.
39. Francis D. Donovan, "Grand Central and Its Predecessors," **The Railway History Monograph,** October 1974, p. 69.
40. Condit, **Port of New York**, vol. 1, p. 93.
41. Geroge W. Hilton, **The Cable Car in America** (Berkeley and Los Angeles, 1971), pp. 299–310.
42. Cunningham and DeHart, **New York City Subway System**, p. 15.
43. Condit, **Port of New York**, vol. 2, p. 6.
44. **Laws of the State of New York**, 1903, May 7.
45. Middleton, **Grand Central**, p. 90.
46. Ibid., p. 82.
47. Michael Batterberry and Ariane Batterberry, **On the Town in New York** (New York, 1973), p. 190. The hotel was demolished during the post-World War II office building boom.
48. **Dun's Review**, February 1946.
49. Pond, **The Golden Earth**, p. 141.
50. Middleton, **Grand Central**, p. 58.
51. Condit, **Port of New York**, vol. 2, pp. 95, 96.
52. "A New Avenue in New York," **The American Architect,** April 3, 1912. The architect making the proposal was Henry Rutgers Marshall.
53. Condit, **Port of New York**, vol. 2, pp. 95, 96.
54. **The New York Times**, 12 October 1919, X 2:3.
55. This was true even though, in this period, the adjacent intersection came to be named Pershing Square, to honor America's wartime general.
56. Ibid., 12 September 1920, VIII, 1:3.
57. W. Parker Chase, **New York, the Wonder City** (New York, 1931), p. 230.
58. Edward Hungerford, "Housekeeping Deluxe," **Tavern Topics,** October 1921, p. 6.
59. Henry Collins Brown, **Valentine's City of New York: A Guide Book** (New York, 1920), p. 276.
60. Chase, **New York, the Wonder City**, p. 276.
61. Ibid., p. 230.
62. Hulbert Footner, **New York City of Cities**, (Philadelphia, 1937), p. 226.
63. Condit, **Port of New York**, vol. 2, pp. 240, 241.
64. Middleton, **Grand Central**, pp. 134, 135.
65. Hungerford, **Tavern Topics**, p. 5.

Elaine Abelson

"Commodore" Cornelius Vanderbilt (1794-1877) by Jared B. Flagg.

■ An architectural symbol of great strength, Grand Central Terminal is also a reminder of that period in American history that has been dubbed the Gilded Age. The spectacular growth of the railroads in post-Civil War America was as much the product of the financial manipulations of a handful of entrepreneurs as it was of the developing new technology. Cornelius Vanderbilt created, owned, and managed the New York Central system. The Central was the "Vanderbilt line," nothing less, and Grand Central Terminal became the tangible expression of the railroad even as it was an architectural and engineering triumph in its own right. In celebrating the preservation of the station, we must not forget the family that was to become part of America's public consciousness for more than a century.

□ Cornelius Vanderbilt, "the Commodore" and founder of the family, epitomized for many of his generation the cherished rags-to-riches myth. Born at the end of the eighteenth century and remembered as a poor, rough-spoken yet intensely ambitious Staten Island ferry boy, Vanderbilt made his initial fortune in steamboats. He viewed the early railroads of the 1830s and 1840s merely as feeders to steamboat traffic.[1] In those decades, railroad lines rarely were longer than fifty miles and either connected existing commercial centers (Philadelphia to Baltimore, Boston to Lowell, New Haven to Hartford, but, ironically, not New Haven to New York) or supplemented existing water transportation.[2] Disconnected stretches of railroad did exist in many of the Eastern Seaboard states, but each was separately owned and separately managed, with varying gauges of track.

□ Rather quickly, however, the speed and all-weather dependability of the railroad became crucial factors in all transportation, and revolutionized travel. Boston to Concord via river and canal took five days upstream and four down in 1840; in 1842, when the Boston & Lowell Railroad reached Concord, "the travel time was cut to four hours one way."[3]

□ Railroads introduced a major innovation in the financing and ownership of transportation companies. Unlike most canals or national roads, most railroads were privately owned; they were far more expensive to build than canals, and required a far greater scale of capitalization than even "the largest textile mills or ironmaking and metal working factories."[4] The capital demands were so great that for the first time funds could not be supplied within single regions. In fact, "soon only the largest financial communities of Europe could provide the vast amounts of capital required,"[5] and railroad bonds, the primary instrument to finance railroad construction, became objects of speculation on an unprecedented scale.

□ The railroad chronicler and analyst, John Moody, considered fiercely competitive Cornelius Vanderbilt the "shrewdest business genius of the day." According to Moody, Vanderbilt was the first man to appreciate the fact that the two leading methods of transportation – steamboats and railroads – were about to change places.[6] Resistant to change, but not inflexibly so, the Commodore eventually became a major participant in the first period of the railroad boom that lasted from the late 1840s to the coming of the depression in the early 1870s.

□ Vanderbilt was not a visionary; he seemed to operate with no single plan. He entered steamboating when its worth and practical value, if not its safety, were obvious, and recognized the potential worth of the railroads only after they had begun to demonstrate their promise. Indifference to established custom and law, combined with a personal bluntness and an uncompromising belief in the use of power when he had it, made Vanderbilt an awesome figure who flourished in the speculative competition for rail routes and franchises. A short note to the managers of his steamship company – who had manipulated stock and gained control while he was in Europe – is typical of Vanderbilt and his methods: "Gentlemen," he wrote, "You have undertaken to cheat me. I will not sue you, for law takes too long. I will ruin you. Sincerely, Cornelius Van Derbilt."[7] (The Dutch spelling was to be Americanized only after the Civil War.)

□ The Vanderbilt railroad ventures began in 1863, when he gained control of the Harlem line, a franchise which was to become the keystone of the whole Central system. Incorporated in 1831 to connect downtown New York with the outlying village of Harlem, the railroad carried largely local passenger traffic and provided a commuting service to southern Westchester. No longer a walking city by the Civil

THE STATUE UNVEILED.

Currier & Ives, 1869.

War, New York had become instead a city of inconvenient distances. Local trains, which stopped at stations along the line from 58th to 125th streets, were an increasingly necessary part of urban transportation.

□ Although burdened with a well-earned reputation as an unattractive business investment, the Harlem had an asset of incalculable value in its right of entry into New York City from the north. Vanderbilt extended its worth still further by obtaining a franchise to operate a streetcar line along Broadway from 42nd Street to the Battery. According to one source, there had been payments of both money and stock to "interested members of the Common Council"[8] for the latter privilege. One clue to future development and the shaping of the urban transportation network lay in the late 1850s decision by the city not to allow street-level steam locomotion south of 42nd Street. It required the railroad to switch from steam, which was noisy and incredibly dirty, to horses before the cars could proceed south into the settled area of Murray Hill. Almost inadvertently, 42nd Street became a central location for the railroad, a transfer point for equipment and passengers.

□ Vanderbilt gained control of the Hudson River Railroad, with its route between Albany and New York City, in 1864; in what was to become standard procedure, he became its president the following year. Together with the Harlem, the Hudson gave Vanderbilt unimpeded access to the city. His major acquisitions were completed in 1867 with the purchase of the New York Central, a continuous one-track line running between Albany and Buffalo. Thus, in less than a decade a vital transportation network was created, with New York City as the focus and Vanderbilt in absolute control. At a time when other overland transportation was at best uncertain, domination of the railroad meant immense personal profits and power. For New York City, already the financial center of the country, it meant even greater preeminence.

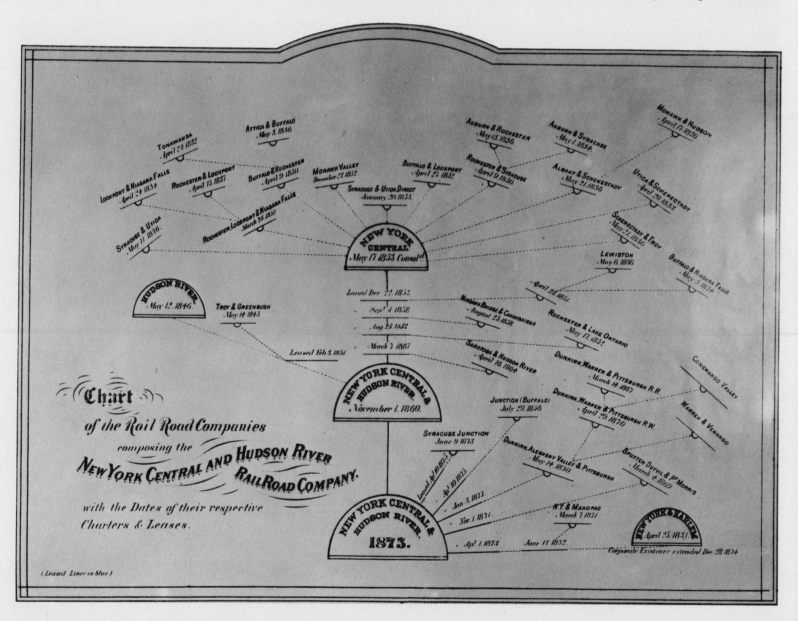

□ Bribery, fraud, collusion, rebates, and manipulation of shipping rates became standard operating practices for both the railroads and their clients in these post-Civil War decades. Not uncommonly, overly susceptible state legislatures, "scoundrelly rings," and an often corrupt judiciary were implicated. In an "Open Letter to Com. Vanderbilt" (just after the so-called Erie Railroad Wars with Jay Gould and Jim Fisk), Mark Twain bitterly lashed out at what he called Vanderbilt's "lawless violations of commercial honor," "The immoral practices, in so prominent a place as you occupy, are a damning example to the rising commercial generation – more, a damning thing to the whole nation." Twain dared the Commodore to act in the public interest:

Go now, and do something that isn't shameful, do go and do something worthy of a man possessed of seventy millions – a man whose most trifling act is remembered and imitated all over the country. . . . You must certainly feel a vague desire in you sometimes to do some splendid deed in the interest of commercial probity or human charity, or of manly honor and dignity.[9]

□ Vanderbilt's business activities must be viewed in light of the general turbulence and low moral tone of the post-Civil War period. Manipulation, dishonesty, and exploitation were accepted business methods in this freewheeling period of rapid railroad expansion, enormous financial opportunities for a select few, and minimal regulation of the new corporate form of business organization. Economic activity was free of all but the most casual restraints. From the 1850s to the end of the century, an "orgy of town-site booms, land grabbing, speculation, railroad booms, financial panics, gold rushes, silver rushes and finally oil rushes repeated themselves decade after decade."[10] As the impact of the railroads became decisive, "whole communities, realizing that the key to economic growth lay in transportation, participated in the mania."[11] Although the laws permitted inflated financing, watered stock predated railroad speculation. The origin of the term was attributed to one Daniel Drew, who supposedly kept his cattle thirsty until immediately before the drovers' market in order to bloat them and thus boost their sale weight. An analyst of the period writes that "Vanderbilt would appear one of the pioneers in the 'watering' of stock upon a scale unknown before him . . . at the time he received legislative right to combine all his roads with the New York Central system, he recapitalized the new corporation at nearly twice its previous market value by ordering a stock dividend of 80 percent."[12]

□ Uneducated and possessed of few social graces, Cornelius Vanderbilt alone created the fortune that succeeding family generations built upon and spent. Although he moved his family from Staten Island to 10 Washington Place in the mid-1840s, he was not himself particularly flamboyant. Racing his trotting horses and gambling at whist were his recreations at Saratoga, where he summered with the wealthy and prominent of his generation. "Most of his personal affairs he handled at an office on West Fourth Street, next door to his stables."[13] A description of this office records a wide table desk with one drawer and an upright desk for his clerk in the corner. He was known for keeping his correspondence and accounts in his head.

□ However, the claims of mere wealth were not yet an acceptable social barometer, and no amount of money ever meant a corresponding elevation in the Commodore's position in society. Vanderbilt was never a drawing room personality. According to Henry Adams, he was "not ornamental," and he decidedly "lacked social charm."[14] Acknowledged as a leading New York citizen – he was selected as a member of the committee for arrangements when the Prince of Wales visited New York in 1860 – he was, nevertheless, condescended to by the social arbiters of his day. An observer noted "The profane and scornful old parvenu Cornelius Van der Bilt was unthinkable in a parlor, but his grandson, William Kissam Vanderbilt, would see all doors open to him in time."[15]

□ As the New York Central grew in both size and carrying capacity, it became evident that terminal facilities in New York City were far from adequate.[16] The railroad solved the freight problem in 1869 by building a block-square three-story terminal and warehouse facility at St. John's Park, south of Canal Street. The site had been owned by Trinity Church and was viewed in some quarters as the "garden spot of downtown, one of the few breathing spaces left to the city poor."[17] The controversy attached to the opening of the building, and particularly to the unveiling of the elaborate bronze work on its pediment, can be glimpsed in the words of Mayor Oakey Hall at the dedication ceremony, and in the outcry that followed.

Cornelius Vanderbilt merit[s] this day marks of public respect and esteem. For his wealth – for the bald reason that he is the richest citizen on this continent? A thousand times, no! . . . Cornelius Vanderbilt has acquired enormous riches. How has he employed them? Not ignobly in selfish investments, nor egotistical accumulations whose income heightens Sybaritish pleasures; not in filling iron chests with title deeds of vast landed estates! But he has used his capital in constant commercial investments.[18]

□ The well-known diarist George Templeton Strong had a different reaction to the idolatry symbolized by "The Bronze."

. . . he is a millionaire of millionaires and, therefore, we bow down before him, and worship him, with a hideous group of molten images, with himself for a central figure, at a cost of $800,000. These be Thy Gods, O Israel!"[19]

A long article in *The Nation* magazine echoed Strong's theme:

There, in the glory of brass are portrayed . . . the trophies of a lineal successor of the medieval baron . . . who was not humanitarian; and not finished in his morals; and not, for his manner, the delight of the refined society of his neighborhood . . . but who knew how to take advantage of lines of travel . . . and who had the heart and hand to levy contributions on all who passed by his way.[20]

VANDERBILT'S OFFICE AT THE GRAND CENTRAL DEPOT.

□ In this single, yet characteristic instance, the justified needs of the railroad combined with Vanderbilt's personal hunger for public glorification and stimulated an outraged response. The bronze work in question was 150 feet long and 30 feet high. On either side were depictions, in high relief, of scenes from Vanderbilt's life. The center niche held the large, free-standing statue of the Commodore that now stands at the front of Grand Central Terminal, facing the automobile ramp and Park Avenue South.

□ A new passenger terminal represented a potentially more complicated, if less controversial, problem for Vanderbilt. The goal was consolidation of the Hudson line, with its main station on 10th Avenue and West 30th Street, with the Harlem, which had tracks and a terminal on Fourth Avenue between 26th and 27th streets. Concluding that the Harlem's east-side entrance into the city was preferable, Vanderbilt decided to connect the Hudson and Harlem by a link outside Manhattan, a five-mile spur enabling both lines to enter the city on the east side and use a single passenger facility. Although not the product of any urban plan, or even centrally located, 42nd Street was the obvious choice for a new depot. To go further downtown ran into the prohibition of steam locomotion in Murray Hill; to go further uptown was just too remote from the city's population centers. Already a railroad transfer point from steam to horses, 42nd was one of the extra-wide crosstown streets; it had east-west traffic, and it was paved with cobblestones.[21] It would be seen only in retrospect that the choice of 42nd Street was a decision that determined the pattern of development for much of New York's east side and culminated in today's Grand Central. The decision would give definitive shape to an area that was to become a transportation, commercial, and cultural axis for the city.

□ Vanderbilt planned the first Grand Central, like the St. John's Park freight depot, as a memorial to himself. "He wanted the largest station in the world," and when it was completed in 1871 it was in fact larger than London's mammoth St. Pancras Station.

Grand Central's five-acre expanse and great vaulted iron arches gave Vanderbilt the personal monument he wanted as well as a substantial capital investment in New York City real estate. The considerable amount of property acquired on what was to become Park Avenue became one of the system's great assets.

□ The second half of the nineteenth century was characterized by rapid industrial and financial concentration and increasing technological efficiency in many areas. Private gain became the surpassing motive for the new, self-styled capitalists as virtue was redefined to encompass financial success. Sanctified by all the major social institutions – schools, churches, the courts, and the federal government, particularly the Senate – the new industrialists became the "dominating figures of an aggressive economic age."[22] Henry Adams sensed the new powers at work in the economy and the deep alterations at work in American society, but, like other social commentators, he was incapable of understanding, much less arresting, what he both feared and despised.

□ Cornelius Vanderbilt exemplified these concerns. During his lifetime he had amassed a personal fortune of unheard-of dimensions, and when he died in January 1877, he was the richest man in America, his wealth surpassing even the fabled fortune of William B. Astor. Vanderbilt died at a critical period in American history, when what many assumed to be an American consensus could visibly be seen to be dissolving, when depression, slums, extreme poverty, rural farm protest, and labor unrest could no longer be ignored, when the urban masses were becoming a noticeable presence for the first time. In attempting to assess the meaning of a public life that stretched back to the era of the first Hudson River steamboats, his obituaries reflected a presentist political orientation. Many newspapers sought a justification of the social order and the economic system in the life of the man.[23] Some saw the honest, sturdy, and fearless individual against the world,[24] the employer to thousands. Others denounced the economic system and condemned Vanderbilt's failure to part with any of his wealth, as at other times they had denounced the way he had accumulated it. It was difficult for them to see how the extraordinary wealth of Vanderbilt squared with American democratic ideology. One Wisconsin paper summed up what many felt when it wrote "that a free government professedly founded on the equal rights of man, can so legislate, as to make it possible for one man to accumulate so much of what other people earned is a reproach."[25]

□ Having founded a dynasty, Vanderbilt had preserved it intact. The bulk of the estate, approximately $90 million, including control of the railroads, went to the oldest son, William Henry. The former Prime Minister of England, William Gladstone, reportedly felt such a fortune "a danger for the people at large, especially when it carried no social obligations to society."[26] For the first time, the amount of money one had and the power it automatically conveyed became a legitimate public concern.

□ The William Henry Vanderbilts conspicuously displayed their newly acquired fortune but failed to gain entry into the innermost circle of New York society. When Mrs. Vanderbilt, in imitation of the governing social elite, laid a red carpet before her door for a reception, society scorned the act as an invasion by social-climbing new money. When their daughter Florence was married in November 1877, *The New York Times* reported that the card for entry into the church caused confusion: "Just inside the outer edge of the canopy stood two rough individuals shouting 'Tickets!' like at a circus." The paper went on to describe the guests inside St. Bartholomew's as a "rather miscellaneous assemblage, in which a large number of Wall Street brokers and members of German banking houses were prominent. There were also many women of a class that would not be expected to receive invitations."[27]

□ It was this second Vanderbilt generation that first moved to Fifth Avenue. As the biographer of August Belmont, the financier, notes, beginning in the 1880s Fifth Avenue became the only correct address for New Yorkers of great wealth and social prestige. The new mansions provided all the public manifestations of recently acquired money. They were purposely designed to enhance the social standing of the nouveau riche. Imported marble and limestone exteriors completely replaced the traditional brownstone as architects and their clients attempted to outdo their counterparts. Six-sixty Fifth, 680, 684, 742, 744, and 746 (better known as 1 West 57th Street) were all Vanderbilt houses, all completed between 1882 and 1892 – the public

William H. Vanderbilt (1821-1885).

Houses of: W. K. Vanderbilt,
architect, R. M. Hunt;
Cornelius Vanderbilt,
architect, George Post;
W. H. Vanderbilt,
architect, Herter Bros.
Harper's Weekly, 1882.

results of the urge for display and the unsurpassed opportunity to create wealth. "Probably never before had a single family dominated so large a stretch of the foremost boulevard of a metropolis."[28]

□ It was, in fact, private commemoration on a scale never before seen in the United States. New heights of extravagance were demonstrated, and ever-new ways of consumption were devised for this "world of triumphant ostentation."[29] The Vanderbilts, and particularly their agents in Europe, physically seized in wholesale batches what Henry James called the spoils of civilization in an attempt to acquire a status and a lineage.[30]

□ A prerequisite for the new grandeur, and as much a symbol of a new social position as a new economic one, was the private art collection and gallery. William H. Vanderbilt was "one of the first in the race for the accumulation of paintings,"[31] a race which enriched a network of dealers and art experts. On occasion Vanderbilt staged "art levees," receptions in his gallery at 660 Fifth Avenue. Twenty-five hundred "gentlemen" were reported at one such event in 1883. Shortly before his death, Vanderbilt's personal collection was valued at over $1.5 million.[32]

□ There *were* other kinds of capitalists. Among the new industrialists were those few who voiced concern over the proper use of their fortunes. While supporting a ruthless system that put great wealth into the hands of a tiny minority as "ordained by the laws of civilization," Andrew Carnegie is, nevertheless, remembered for his philanthropy, not his private expenditures. Men should not die rich, he wrote in the *Gospel of Wealth*; rather, they should act as trustees for the community, and use their wealth during their lifetimes for socially useful purposes.[33] The Carnegie Fund and thousands of free public libraries have testified to Carnegie's principles in practice. In their philanthropy as in their lives, the Vanderbilts represented quite a different philosophy.

□ The Commodore had disapproved of most forms of charity, and, with the exception of Vanderbilt University, he made few donations. William, on the other hand, made substantial gifts, but only to the established cultural institutions – the Metropolitan Museum of Art, The Museum of Natural History, Columbia College of Physicians and Surgeons. Somewhat quixotically, he also provided funds for the erection in Central Park of the Obelisk of Thothmes that became known as Cleopatra's Needle. Here was an embellishment of the city that everyone could see and approve. At the dedication ceremony in February 1881, Vanderbilt was presented with a medal to commemorate the event. The citation read:

Presented to the United States by Ismail Khedive of Egypt, 1881. Quarried at Syrene and erected at Heliopolis by Thothmes III. Re-erected at Alexandria under Augustus. Removed to New York through the liberality of W. H. Vanderbilt. . . .[34]

□ After the death of his father, William H. Vanderbilt became the single powerful force in the New York Central. Although the main routes of the railroad had been established earlier, the system grew in the 1880s to far beyond any point the Commodore could have envisioned. Cornelius Vanderbilt initially had opposed the railroad's going west of Buffalo, feeling he "might as well go to San Francisco and China,"[35] but the race for markets provided its own impetus, and the system expanded inexorably – north to Toronto, south to St. Louis, and west through Chicago as far as Omaha.[36]

□ William Vanderbilt's short career as sole operating head of the Central was coincidental with the first great railroad strike in the United States. As wages dropped and working conditions appreciably worsened during the economic decline of the 1870s, the railroad workers became increasingly militant. A work stoppage on the Baltimore & Ohio in July 1877 spread within days to other lines across the county. Demanding the restoration of a 10 percent wage reduction, the strikers on parts of the New York Central system appealed directly to Vanderbilt, who, as was his habit, was summering at the United States Hotel in Saratoga. Vanderbilt not only refused to recognize the strikers as his men ("The shops have been visited by a mob and my men have been forced to quit work"),[37] he justified the wage cuts as part of the emergencies of the business situation ("We have simply done what we have been obliged to do and they [the men] comprehend this thoroughly").[38] Vanderbilt also referred to the strikers as belonging to "the Communistic classes and manifesting a disposition to pillage and destroy private property."[39] According to *The New York Times,* brakemen, who averaged $2.15 for a 150-mile trip, had been reduced to $1.90; conductors' wages had gone down from $2.87 to $2.60.[40]

□ Cushioned by his wealth and insulated by subservience, Vanderbilt's callousness was typical. In what may be a classic statement by a self-proclaimed capitalist and inheritor of the largest fortune in the United States, he told a *Times* reporter at the conclusion of the strike:

Our men feel that although I may own the majority of the stock in the Central, my interests are as much affected in degree as are theirs; and although I may have my millions and they have the rewards of their daily toil, still we are about equal in the end.[41]

□ Not until the beginning of the 1880s did adverse public opinion become even a slight influence on the railroad's financial management. When William Vanderbilt announced to a New York State legislative investigating committee that he was "personally the owner of over 87 percent of the hundred million capital of the company,"[42] public indignation was so great – and the possibility of state interference in railroad operations so threatening – that Vanderbilt found it prudent to divest himself of some of his holdings. The investment banker Pierpont Morgan was brought in and arranged a private sale in England to dispose of a portion of Vanderbilt's New York Central stock. It was at this point that the close identification of the Vanderbilt railroads with Morgan began. He became an active member of the board of directors of the New York Central and, according to the analyst John Moody, ultimately the real financial power behind the Vanderbilt system.[43] At the same time, the Vanderbilts themselves became increasingly less active and visible in the railroad's management.

□ William H. Vanderbilt died in December 1885. Having doubled – some maintained trebled – the Commodore's fortune in seven years, he was perceived to be the richest man in the world, with a fortune surpassed only by "the aggregate wealth of all the Rothschilds combined."[44] Whatever the amount, manipulation of railroad properties had yielded the Vanderbilts a colossal fortune. Cornelius Vanderbilt II, the oldest of William's eight children, became titular head of the House of Vanderbilt, a house which, by this third generation, had acquired a coat of arms that consisted of three acorns and a motto: Great oaks from little acorns grow.[45]

House of William Kissam Vanderbilt.
Architect: Richard Morris Hunt.

□ Following the inheritance pattern established by the Commodore, the bulk of the estate remained intact, passed on to the two oldest sons, Cornelius and William Kissam, who exercised control, respectively, through the offices of chairman of the board and president of the major Vanderbilt railroads. It was understood, however, that the working head was Cornelius. "Goaded by the social ambitions of his wife, Alva Murray Smith of Mobile, William Kissam was much more interested in society."[46]

□ The 1880s and 1890s were the age of the new moneyed society in New York. Not Edith Wharton's true Knickerbocker society, these were the new people, the consumers, the suddenly rich who attempted to buy social preeminence.[47] Mrs. William Astor was the unchallenged social arbiter, and Ward McAllister was her protégé. It was into this rigid, hierarchical, grossly material world that Mr. and Mrs. William K. Vanderbilt charged in what became a relentless campaign for status and social recognition.

□ Alva Smith Vanderbilt was by all accounts the most socially competitive of all the Vanderbilt women. The recollections of the time are laden with references to her towering ambition, to her craving what one account described as "a residence with a design so stunning that no one would refuse her invitations."[48] The biographer of architect Richard Morris Hunt writes, "clearly Alva Smith Vanderbilt undertook to direct the design of the new Fifth Avenue mansion ('a little Chateau de Blois,' she called it[49]), as she did to establish her own social position and to dominate the destinies of her children."[50] In the battle to erect "the largest and grandest mansion . . . the most elaborate, most expensive monument of financial success,"[51] Alva and William led the way. The lavishness and grandeur of their urban chateau at 660 Fifth Avenue can only be imagined: Some say it was the loveliest of the Fifth Avenue mansions. Alva capped her successful campaign for social recognition with a costume housewarming ball for 1,200 people in March 1883, which was described in *The New York Herald* as "presenting a scene probably never rivaled in Republican America."[52]

□ In this consuming attempt to articulate a personal grandeur, the city was the ultimate victor. Fifth Avenue became permanently associated with the "best" – the best people, the best shops, and the best address. Ironically, none of the Vanderbilt mansions, which did so much to confirm this status, survive.

□ New York City played a special role in the America of this period. Easily the largest city in the country, with a population of almost 1.5 million, New York was an attraction in the "opportunities afforded for men of ability, but also by its imperial wealth,

117

its Parisian, indeed almost sybaritic luxury, and its social splendor."[53] So writes Henry Clews, a financier who chronicled the age. Clews becomes positively effusive in describing the city.

. . . the glitter of peerless fashion, the ceaseless roll of splendid equipages, and the Bois de Boulogne of America, the Central Park; here there is a constant round of brilliant banquets, afternoon teas and receptions . . . the grand balls with their more formal pomp and splendid circumstances. . . . It does not take much of this kind of life to make enthusiastic New Yorkers of the wives of western millionaires, and then nothing remains but to purchase a brownstone mansion, and swing into the tide of fashion with receptions, balls and kettle-drums, elegant equipages with coachmen in bright buttoned livery, footmen in top boots, maid-servants and man-servants, including a butler and all the other adjuncts of fashionable life in the great metropolis.[54]

According to Ward McAllister, a fortune of a million was now nothing; one needed a fortune of ten, fifty, one hundred million to be counted rich.[55]

□ Another symbol of the financial and social power of the nouveau riche was the new Metropolitan Opera House. Refused any of the eighteen boxes at the Academy of Music on Irving Place and 14th Street, and ultimately unwilling to compromise with the old aristocracy, the so-called new Medici[56] founded the Metropolitan Opera Company and erected their own opera house uptown at 39th Street and Broadway. In an unequivocal showdown with old New York society, the sheer prestige represented by the new opera forced the Academy of Music company to disband within two years. The Schuylers, Beekmans, Livingstons, and Bayards gave way to the Vanderbilts, Goelets, Whitneys, Goulds, Morgans, Drexels, and Rockefellers. An organizer of the new institution and a leading stockholder, William K. Vanderbilt was listed as owning three boxes when the Met opened in October 1883.[57]

□ The history of the Vanderbilts of this third generation could easily be written in the history of their residential architecture. The Breakers of Cornelius II and Marble House of William Kissam, the families' so-called cottages at Newport, established it as the most fashionable resort in the United States in the 1890s. The motivations for building these visible trophies of their financial power were complex – social competitiveness and personal ambition surely occupy some part of the rationale. Perhaps, too, the houses were in emulation of the European tradition, where "high social position . . . was usually associated with elegant residences."[58] Descriptions of the Newport "cottages" focus on their size (seventy rooms at The Breakers), the lavishness and grandeur of their design and furnishings, and the entertainments that took place in them. Many social critics found the extravagant display appalling[59] and senseless, "irrelevant to much of American life."[60] The ultimate monument of Gilded Age extravagance, and the last great Vanderbilt house, was Biltmore, a French-styled chateau set on 125,000 acres in Asheville, North Carolina. Created by George Vanderbilt and the architect Richard Morris Hunt, Biltmore was to be Renaissance Europe in an American setting.

□ The marriage of William K. and Alva's daughter Consuelo to Charles Richard John Spencer-Churchill, the ninth Duke of Marlborough, capped the Vanderbilts' social ambitions. In one of several trans-Atlantic society marriages of the 1890s, the great-granddaughter of the first Cornelius Vanderbilt married into the highest level of the English peerage, supported by a family settlement that was generous even by the exaggerated standards of 1895. Walter Damrosch, leader of the New York Symphony, led the sixty members of the orchestra at St. Thomas Episcopal Church. (The Vanderbilts' Moravian affiliation had been dropped years earlier as the Episcopal Church became the choice of the majority of the rich and the social.) After days of elaborate coverage of the engagement and the wedding preparations, *The New York Times* described the finale: "The wedding yesterday was without exception the most magnificent ever celebrated in this country, which was quite fitting, in view of the great wealth and social position of the bride and the high rank of the bridegroom."[61] Quite a change in tone from the reporting of the first Vanderbilt society wedding in 1877! Guests included the Governor of New York and Mrs. Levi P. Morton, Mr. and Mrs. John Jacob Astor, *the* Mrs. William Astor, Colonel and Mrs. William Jay, and

British Ambassador Sir Julian Pauncefote. Conspicuously absent from the wedding were most of the Vanderbilts. Alva and William had just been involved in the "first major divorce of American society,"[62] and none but the bride's immediate family would make a public appearance with Alva.

□ Cornelius and William K. Vanderbilt were nominally head of the New York Central System, but, increasingly, their role was a passive one. At the time of Cornelius's death in 1899, William was living abroad and making only infrequent business trips to the United States. The system's real operating head was Chauncey Depew, a one-time Vanderbilt lobbyist in Albany, former vice-president for railroad legal affairs, president of the New York Central in the 1890s, and by the turn of the century United States Senator from New York. When Cornelius died, Depew took over as chairman. Although William was chosen president, his participation was short-lived. In 1903 *The New York Times* explained that the Vanderbilts had voluntarily surrendered their position: "For some time," the article allowed, "William K. Vanderbilt has found the management of these great properties irksome and confining," and it was his "wish" to be relieved of his responsibilities and "his exacting duties."[63] For the first time since 1863, no Vanderbilt was part of the railroad's operating management.[64]

□ Even though Vanderbilts continued for some time to be the largest stockholders and were well represented on the board of directors, executive leadership was provided by others. When William Rockefeller, and later Edward Harriman, of the Union Pacific went on the Central board, it signaled the end of family management and nepotism based on ownership. Only William Kissam II, the older son of William K. and Alva, actively represented the fourth generation on the Vanderbilt roads. But this William never achieved the controlling position that earlier Vanderbilt generations had naturally assumed. The Vanderbilt line was, in fact, no longer that.

□ What explains this precipitous departure from a giant transportation network? The loss of absolute control? The failure of that ruthless competitive instinct which possessed the Commodore? A slackening of the compelling need to prove oneself and the family to the world? The reasons are debatable, but the results are unambiguous. The family's active connection with the railroad became more and more tangential, until a House committee investigating the major shareholdings in American railroads in 1931 found that the Vanderbilt family held only slightly more than 4.5 percent of the issued stock and voting power and were second to the Union Pacific's 5.5 percent. The report concluded that "large individual or family holdings of railroad securities appear to be quite limited."[65]

□ The need for a totally new Grand Central was evident even as the Commodore's personal monument was being remodelled at the turn of the century. Passenger traffic had increased substantially, and the old terminal was clearly inadequate. Newly developed electric technology became the key element in a radically new design that eliminated both the persistent ventilation problem and the street-level fatalities caused by the part-open-cut, part-tunnel arrrangement that was the legacy of the Grand Central of the 1870s. Plans for the new station became part of a broader scheme for development of the whole area around Park Avenue and 42nd Street, an ambitious urban plan which included apartments, office buildings, and hotels built on the valuable air rights over the unsightly switching yards, railroad shops, and tracks.

□ Only through Whitney Warren, a cousin and close friend of William K. Vanderbilt II, is it possible to perceive any direct family connection to the terminal. Although Reed and Stem, the architectural firm originally chosen for the design, was persuaded after the fact to associate with the Warren and Wetmore firm, there are no clear links between the Vanderbilts and the modern Grand Central. The family seems to have been conspicuously uninvolved.

□ Assessing the Vanderbilts is not an easy task. They cannot be personally faulted for the gross inequalities spawned by industrial capitalism. They must be viewed in light of an economic system and ideology that reflected an earlier period, a commercial, not an industrial America. For several decades railroads were the largest business enterprises in the world, and during this time laissez-faire economics only slowly began to be challenged by those demanding control of the new hydra.

William Kissam Vanderbilt II (1878-1944).

□ In a very real sense, the Commodore and his son William Henry were creators. They built the system and created the wealth that succeeding generations displayed, fought over, and used to commemorate themselves. What did the Vanderbilts see as the obligations of this wealth? A difficult question to answer. Certainly the high cultural institutions of society benefited – the museums, churches, and universities. But the Carnegie concept of obligation, in the sense of duty to others, was not apparent in most of their public benefactions. If the Vanderbilts believed that wealth obliged them to social consciousness, there was little evidence of this in their self-celebrating activities.

□ What of their civic consciousness? The Commodore constructed the first Grand Central Station as an intensely personal legacy, even as it was a public facility. Unquestionably, the Fifth Avenue mansions were examples of nineteenth-century architecture at its most creative. The William K. Vanderbilt house at 660 Fifth Avenue and the Cornelius Vanderbilt house at 1 West 57th Street were models of grandeur that greatly contributed to the perception of Fifth Avenue as the central, most elegant thoroughfare in the city. It is problematical, however, whether these private structures can be equated with civic consciousness. The Vanderbilts were, finally, unwitting shapers of the city, for regardless of their motives, they were responsible for monumental structures that gave civic significance to urban space.

□ The present Grand Central is an urban vision of a very different sort. It was planned and built in the twentieth century, at a time when the family had withdrawn both from active management in the railroad and from being a creative economic force in the city. Paradoxically, perhaps, removed as it was from the era of the family's heyday, the station was the culmination of that quest for permanent civic grandeur whose beginnings can be traced to a more conscious architectural and urban tradition. Whatever debt is owed to the family remains intangible.

1. Wheaton J. Lane, **Commodore Vanderbilt** (New York, 1942), p. 73.
2. Alfred D. Chandler, Jr., **The Visible Hand** (Cambridge, Mass., 1977), p. 82.
3. Ibid., p. 86.
4. Ibid., p. 90.
5. Ibid., p. 91.
6. John Moody, **The Railroad Builders, A Chronicle of the Welding of the States** (New Haven, 1919), vol. 38, p. 13.
7. Matthew Josephson, **The Robber Barons** (New York, 1934), p. 15.
8. Ibid., p. 68.
9. Mark Twain, "Open Letter to Com. Vanderbilt," **Packard's Monthly I**, 1869, pp. 89–91.
10. Josephson, **Robber Barons**, p. 25.
11. Samuel P. Hays, **The Response to Industrialism: 1885–1914** (Chicago, 1957), p. 6.
12. Josephson, **Robber Barons**, p. 72.
13. Lane, **Commodore Vanderbilt**, p. 164.
14. Henry Adams, **The Education of Henry Adams** (Boston, 1961), p. 238.
15. Josephson, **Robber Barons**, p. 239.
16. Lane, **Commodore Vanderbilt**, p. 281.
17. **The Diary of George Templeton Strong**, vol. 4: **Post-War Years, 1865–1875**, eds. Allan Nevins and Milton Halsey Thomas (New York, 1952), p. 108.
18. **New York Daily Tribune**, 11 November 1869.
19. Strong, **Diary**, p. 259.
20. **The Nation**, "The Vanderbilt Memorial," November 18, 1869, p. 431.
21. Lane, **Commodore Vanderbilt**, p. 282.
22. Josephson, **Robber Barons**, vii.
23. Sigmund Diamond, **The Reputation of American Businessmen** (Cambridge, Mass., 1955), p. 54.
24. Ibid., p. 57.
25. **Sparta Wisconsin Greenback**, 11 January 1877, quoted in Diamond, **The Reputation**, p. 66.
26. Josephson, **Robber Barons**, p. 183.
27. **The New York Times**, 22 November 1877.
28. Alan Churchill, **The Splendor Seekers** (New York, 1974), p. 71.
29. Ibid., p. 46.
30. Josephson, **Robber Barons**, p. 341.
31. Ibid.
32. Wayne Andrews, **The Vanderbilt Legend** (New York, 1941), p. 223.
33. Andrew Carnegie, **The Gospel of Wealth and Other Timely Essays**, ed. Edward C. Kirkland (Cambridge, Mass., 1962), pp. 20–25.
34. **The New York Times**, 23 February 1881.
35. Josephson, **Robber Barons**, p. 73.
36. Moody, **Railroad Builders**, p. 36.
37. **The New York Times**, 25 July 1877.
38. Ibid., 24 July 1877.
39. Ibid., 25 July 1877.
40. Ibid., 26 July 1877.
41. Ibid., 28 July 1877.
42. Moody, **Railroad Builders**, p. 36.
43. John Moody, **The Masters of Capital, A Chronicle of Wall Street** (New Haven, 1919). vol. 41, p. 32.
44. Henry Clews, **Twenty-Eight Years in Wall Street** (New York, 1908), p. 351.
45. Andrews, **Vanderbilt Legend**, p. 286.
46. B. H. Friedman, **Gertrude Vanderbilt Whitney** (New York, 1978), p. 16.
47. Churchill, **Splendor Seekers**, p. 97.
48. Ibid., p. 59.
49. Friedman, **Gertrude Vanderbilt Whitney**, p. 16.
50. Paul R. Baker, **Richard Morris Hunt** (Cambridge, Mass., 1980), p. 275.
51. **The American Renaissance 1876–1917** (The Brooklyn Museum, 1979), p. 120.
52. **New York Herald**, 27 March 1883.
53. Henry Clews, **Fifty Years in Wall Street** (New York, 1980), p. 449.
54. Ibid.
55. Ward McAllister, **Society As I Have Found It** (New York, 1890), p. 349.
56. Lloyd Morris, **Incredible New York** (New York, 1951), p. 191.
57. **The New York Times**, 24 May 1883.
58. Baker, **Richard Morris Hunt**, p. 334.
59. Ibid., p. 372.
60. Ibid., p. 432.
61. **The New York Times**, 6 November 1895.
62. Churchill, **Splendor Seekers**, p. 62.
63. **The New York Times**, 25 March 1903.
64. **Poor's Directory of Railway Officials and Railway Directors, 1891–1903**.
65. U. S. Congress, House, **Regulation of Stock Ownership in Railroads**, H.R. 2789, 71st Cong., 3rd Sess., 1931, LXIX.

Milton R. Newman

■ It's unfortunate that, when Andy Warhol was turning out multiple images of Marilyn and Elvis back in the sixties, he didn't throw in a few of Grand Central Station. We have seen Grand Central, like the movie and rock stars, so often and for so long that it has become invisible – an icon that is taken for granted as much by those who have never even seen it as it is by those who use it every day. We need a Warhol (Donald Trump?) to wrench it out of context, paint it garish colors, and force us, finally, to see it again. We need to rehear its stories and relearn its lessons about city-building before the city builds itself into hopeless chaos.

□ It would be fortuitous if this exhibition could serve such a function, since it comes at a time when a new spurt of building in Manhattan threatens to obliterate the last vestiges of this city's rough, distinctive, and barely restrained beauty. If we can rediscover Grand Central, like a box forgotten in the attic, we will find stored away inside the tools needed to build constructively again.

□ The true rediscovery of Grand Central, however, cannot be just a matter of pointing a spotlight at it and investing it with superstar status. It is all too easy to see Grand Central as just an isolated phenomenon: It is an old, low building increasingly surrounded by new skyscrapers; its functions are so specialized that only three or four other buildings in the entire city are even roughly comparable; and the campaign to have it designated as a landmark has stressed its uniqueness above all else. But the real distinction of Grand Central lies not in its unusual aspects, but in precisely those features and functions that it shares with all buildings: its relationships to the city, the street, and the people who pass through and around it. Although there have been buildings which worked as well in some respects, there has been no other I know as successful at all levels of interaction as Grand Central. And this success comes not from style or function or historical accident, but from a broad sensitivity to the way cities, and buildings, work. Thus, if Grand Central is a box of urban tools, the key to that box is a basic understanding of what the concept of "city" means.

The Atomization of the City

□ It used to be that a city was an animal and buildings were its cells. This was the case from the time cities began until sometime around the 1940s when, quite suddenly, the individual building became the primary unit – the animal – and the city became a herd of buildings. Buildings began to acquire their own little parks, police forces, climates, communications, and even power supply systems, all of which, and more, were previously shared on a city-wide basis. The change was initially a conceptual one, appearing in the 1920s in the writings and sketches of Le Corbusier and others, but within a decade the drawings started to be-

come real, and by 1961 a sweeping revision of New York City's zoning regulations embodied the new attitude and hastened its spread.

□ Although this process took place within what was, historically, a relatively short time span, it was gradual enough so that the accompanying problems were entrenched and extensive before we even began to recognize them as problems. In fact it is only in the last year or two that New York's city planners have started to address the situation, with zoning changes designed to produce squat, street-hugging buildings, a progressive step which is overshadowed by the fact that it seems to represent a mere treatment of symptoms without any real awareness of the underlying disease.

□ It is beyond the scope of this essay to travel to the sources of this urban malady, but a short excursion in that direction may be useful. Without attempting to separate cause and effect, we can observe that the change coincided with a substitution of private interests for those of the community as the first priority in the most basic urban design decisions. It may be that big business was more powerful in the past, and there have always been corporations and individuals prepared to erect a new building as a personal symbol or monument. But this always took place in a city that had a stylistic identity of its own, to which the new building invariably paid its respects even while trying to transcend it. (The Flatiron Building, however revolutionary it may have been in technology, shape, or size, still struck several familiar chords with its ornate stone facade.)○And there was a much simpler re-

lationship then between corporate aspirations and civic significance. Grand Central, for example, was erected in truly grand style by a huge corporation, no doubt to embellish its own image and build its profits, but these goals dovetailed nicely with the civic importance of the city's major terminal, as well as with the immense functional, and consequently symbolic, significance to the society of the time. Similarly, the AT&T (the original one at 195 Broadway), Chrysler (405 Lexington Avenue), or Woolworth (233 Broadway)○buildings were, simultaneously, corporate monuments and symbolic temples of Communications, Industry, and Commerce, respectively. And they were distinctive, even radical, while retaining enough of a link to their surroundings – through the use of material, massing, and scale – to fit in as parts of a larger whole, rather than standing as little self-contained and self-referential universes.

□ It might seem at first that the proliferation of corporate giants made some kind of urban conceptual change inevitable. It is easy to let AT&T symbolize communications, but what is to happen when IT&T and Comsat and CBS want buildings too? And what are Lever Brothers or American Can Company to represent in our pantheon of corporate and urban imagery? Well, there have always been the anonymous buildings and the Nuts & Bolts Corp. headquarters, content to take their places among the large majority of urban structures which have always provided a varied but coherent backdrop to the action. Now all it takes is some brash new real estate developer or fast-growing conglomerate and we are confronted with yet another glass-and-chrome extravaganza fighting to win our attention away from the building across the street. Everybody wants to be in the foreground.

□ The modern or international movement has not helped either, and it was inevitable that its expressions of new construction technologies would create some unfortunate urban confrontations. But even these could have been minimized, if the will had been there, as is evident from the few exceptional cases like Butterfield House (37 W. 12th Street)○or the Guardian Life Insurance Building (305 E. 17th Street).○The design professions, however, for reasons of survival or ego or both, have enthusiastically embraced the shift in urban emphasis, and have uncritically adopted the new technologies and styles as convenient expressions thereof.

□ All of these factors have contributed to a "me generation" of buildings, and the corresponding loss of a sense of the whole in our cities. Perhaps they are just reverberations of more complex postindustrial, postspiritual changes in our society's self-image. Whatever the causes, it would be fruitless to try and retrace our steps back to some urban Eden. We can learn from our mistakes, however, and perhaps do better in the future than we have in the recent past. This means abandoning the simplistic, quick-fix gimmicks that have become all too familiar: the special zoning districts, design controls, and other forms of design by fiat, committee, and bureaucracy. We must do nothing less than reacquire a sense of the city as a single organism, and we could have no better starting place for this task than Grand Central.

The Responsibilities of an Urban Building

□ When cities were organisms, individual buildings, like cells in an animal or citizens in a state, had certain responsibilities to the common corporate purpose. Each building had obligations on three planes: to its occupants, to passers-by, and to the city as a whole. This layered existence – inside/outside/symbol or even mind/body/spirit – was such a basic given in times past that it was never even stated. It was an understanding that came with living in the city, like how to keep from falling over in a lurching subway or how to recognize the beginning of spring without ever seeing trees or grass. Those who designed buildings and cities for a living knew it even better, although for them, too, it was so obvious as to be trivial. And perhaps it was just because it was so completely taken for granted that the concept could slip away so quickly.

□ In fact it was this very ability of buildings to function simultaneously on the smallest and largest scale – like a molecule of soap bonding at one end with grease and at the other with water – that gave the city its cohesiveness. Naturally, then, the conceptual structure of the city and that of the individual building had to deteriorate together, so that now, in an increasingly amorphous city, we see buildings with no symbolic resonances whatsoever, and with what is essentially no inside, or no outside, or often both. As paradoxical as this may sound, it becomes quite clear when we compare Grand Central with some recent structures.

Inside/Outside

□ It might seem unnecessary to specify that every building must have an inside and an outside, but consider the new Citicorp building at 153 E. 53rd Street. Inside there appears to be plenty going on: The central atrium is crammed with shops, escalators, seating, and all manner of architectural detail.○But outside on the sidewalk there is . . . nothing.○The exterior of the building is essentially blank walls: no shops, no real show windows, and no embellishment. On the other hand, at 850 Third Avenue the reverse occurs. Shops and windows enliven the sidewalk,○but inside there is nothing but featureless marble and, with luck, a newsstand tucked in some odd corner.

□ The logical conclusion of this trend has, of course, already been reached with buildings like the Seagram's (375 Park Avenue) which, whatever their architectural merits, have neither inside○nor outside○as far as the average pedestrian is concerned. In this company, even Citicorp begins to look warm and comfortably old-fashioned.

□ Contrast such examples with Grand Central, which is lined, inside○and out○with all manner of events: shops,○windows,○ public conveniences (seats, phones, toilets),○and architectural ornament.○ It generates its own vibrant environment, interior and exterior, thereby giving back to the city more energy than it absorbs, and illuminating the fact that many recent buildings are little more than energy-absorbing black holes. One of the largest and most successful examples of this urban symbiosis is Rockefeller Center, but it should not be concluded that size and complexity are essential to constructive interaction with the city. Two ninety-five Madison Avenue is a relatively modest office building (it is quite high, but only 50 feet wide), but it stylishly achieves similar results. The long lobby is brought to life by dramatic architectural features○and a succession of shops, many of which do double duty by opening onto the adjacent sidewalks as well.○,○

□ It is not enough, however, just to sprinkle shops or seating or other amenities around. They must be located so as to have some natural relationship to the people who they are to serve. In Grand Central the amenities are concentrated along the most intensely used pedestrian paths, namely the train and subway access passages and the sidewalks fronting on 42nd Street and Lexington Avenue. It all works so well that the real complexities of what is occurring are not immediately apparent.

□ The streets are the key to any city. It is the quality of experience there that determines whether a city has the dynamic feeling which we have come to think of as urban, or the more relaxed, passive atmosphere associated with the rural, or suburban. The difference lies not in the kinds of activity taking place, or even in the volume of traffic, but in the physical relationship between activities.

In a nonurban situation, things tend to be neatly compartmentalized, with clear definition of the proscribed location for each street function.

□ A truly urban street, by comparison, is a mess. Although it can be analyzed in terms of four basic functions, corresponding to four zones, these zones are not clearly defined, but blend and overlap in a constantly changing pattern.○Closest to the building line is the realm of window-shoppers, people going in and out of stores (and lobbies), and people just standing or sitting around. The middle of the sidewalk is for the walkers. Near the curb is another strip for sitters and standers, also used by those entering or leaving vehicles or crossing the street. And finally there is the portion reserved for vehicles. The resulting mix can become uncomfortable, even dangerous, at times as the volume of pedestrians or traffic increases, but it is this very concentration, of both function and form, and the overlapping that results, which make the city special. It is a simultaneity and spontaneity which permit a pedestrian to window-shop, buy a hot dog, and meet a friend, all in the same 100-foot by 12-foot strip of sidewalk between the bus stop and the office.

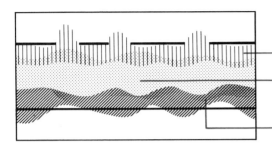

□ As our cities have deteriorated, we have seen a lot of tinkering with this traditional street mix. Apparently there is some rudimentary understanding that the character of the streets is critical to the well-being of the city, but frequently this proposition has been reversed to produce the unfortunate corollary that any urban problem can be solved by manipulating the street. Thus, the street zones have been increasingly isolated or eliminated, and we have been given streets without vehicles (pedestrian malls);○ streets without people walking (multilevel separation of functions);○streets without people sitting or standing around (vest-pocket parks);○and streets without shops or windows (plazas○and projects). ○The results have almost always been depressing, but somehow the same old ideas keep getting dusted off and recycled.

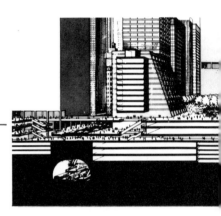

□ The sterility of these gambits is thrown into sharp relief by the richness of the approach taken at Grand Central, which treats the station's special transportation functions like added zones of street activity, overlapping with and enriching the mix of the other four. Rather than presenting a formal, remote facade like the old Penn Station,○ Grand Central embraced the street and interacted with it, lining the sidewalk with a lively mix of shops, pedestrian and vehicular entrances to the station, and entrances to the subways. (Interestingly, Grand Central's designers recognized that it was possible to have too much of a good thing, and elevated Park Avenue at that point. Interrupting it would have created vehicular chaos, and leaving it at ground level would have isolated the station between two rivers of

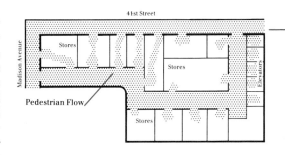

through traffic.) While this approach sometimes seems to skirt confusion, even confusion seems preferable to the dullness of, say, Sixth Avenue in the 40s, where all of the street functions have been neatly separated: buildings set back from the street behind plazas, ○seating in more plazas behind them,○and stores in an underground passageway. The hapless pedestrian can either stick to the sidewalk, with only the traffic for entertainment, or make a series of detours to sit, shop, or look in a window.

□ Inside a building the mix is – or can be – comparable to what it is outside, minus the cars and trucks, but few buildings recognize that fact anymore. If amenities are provided at all, they are given their own little zones, while the main pedestrian paths, usually between the elevators and the street, are left as bare as a men's room and about as stimulating (the General Motors Building at 767 Fifth Avenue).○At the Citicorp building great attention has been given to providing interior amenities, but because they are encapsulated in their own separate area, they have an essentially passive, unspontaneous, and therefore profoundly suburban character. The building was laid out so that the large majority of the people working in it would enter from the west – because that is where the subway is – and go up in the elevators without ever passing the shops. And since the shops are not visible from the street, and the path through the building does not serve as a shortcut to anywhere, most of the shops' patrons have made a conscious decision to go there, and a detour to get there. The result is, in fact, nothing but a suburban shopping mall, although the price level of the shops is high enough to eliminate many of the building's own office workers as customers, and both the food-related nature of most of the shops and their similarity of function tend to eliminate shopping in the "browsing" sense of the word.○

□ Grand Central does precisely the opposite. It recognizes the paths of greatest pedestrian flow – access to trains and subways – and that is where it concentrates its amenities. It creates an environment with the same overlapping zones as on a sidewalk (minus vehicles), and thereby permits a commuter to take the same train every day for twenty years and still have something slightly new and useful to greet him at the beginning or end of his trip: a cup of coffee at Nedicks; something to read at The Open Book; a new display at Hoffritz; a new store where the movie theater used to be; a new picture on the Kodak sign; and, of course, the newspaper. All of these diversions, and many more, are available without detouring from the shortest, quickest path between train and office, and often without even breaking stride.○

Design and Myth

Placement

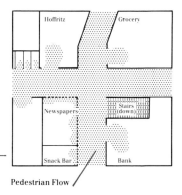

Pedestrian Flow

□ Here, too, it is useful to look at other buildings, such as 249 Madison,○the Lincoln Building (60 W. 42nd Street), or the Chanin Building (122 E. 42nd Street), to remind us that it doesn't take a particularly large or complex building like Grand Central or Radio City to provide amenities or to put them where they can do the most good. Such buildings are, in fact, fairly numerous, particularly within a few blocks of Grand Central but also in the Wall Street area. They are all stylistically dated, but few if any of the shops serving their sidewalks or lobbies are vacant. Maybe the economic moral is even more significant than the urban design moral. Or maybe, in this case at least, good economics and good design are the same thing.

□ The three aspects of a building – interior, exterior, and conceptual – are not entirely distinct, but tend to shade from one to the next like colors in a spectrum. The first two are primarily functional, with visual components, while the last is essentially the reverse, and because of this limited involvement with function the conceptual facet is the trickiest to understand and evaluate. Its potential impact on the city, however, is the greatest of the three since it combines the inherent power of myth with the fact that buildings are among the largest fabricated objects, and since it can operate simultaneously on several different symbolic levels. The conceptual/symbolic/mythical component of Grand Central successfully spans almost all of these levels, and permits us to examine them individually, starting with the first symbolic decision which has to be made for every new building: placement.

□ As one of the city's two rail centers, Grand Central is a full-fledged civic landmark, and its placement makes this instantly evident (in contrast, of course, to the "new" Penn Station, which is totally underground, and has no civic presence at all). Grand Central's axial siting at the end of Park Avenue's long vista announces the fact that this is not just another ordinary building with a commonplace function. And since it straddles several cross-streets, it is also highly visible from east and west, despite the fact that it is lower than the surrounding buildings. This visual prominence makes it not only a navigational reference point for pedestrians and motorists, but also a natural focus for the central midtown area, thereby again reinforcing its symbolic stature.○,○

□ A number of other New York buildings have used this traditional placement device to declare symbolically their civic importance – the Municipal Building (1 Centre Street),○the Public Library (at Fifth Avenue and 42nd Street),○the old Penn Station – and in all these it is clearly appropriate. As the old concept of the city dissolved, however, buildings began to usurp civic prominence by using the same tricks of placement formerly reserved for a small elite. The Pan Am Building at 200 Park Avenue is probably the most visible of these,○but many of the "urban renewal" housing projects were also sited so as to take on an apparent symbolic importance, which was exaggerated by their large size, despite being simultaneously contradicted by the banality of their design.○

Size

□ Sheer size, of course, can be enough to generate mythic status by itself. The Empire State Building (350 Fifth Avenue) is, after all, just another office building, but its size made it an instant icon.○(Whether this would have happened if it had not been centrally located and of some design distinction we will never know, but it seems to be more than holding its own in the symbol department against competition from the World Trade Center, with location and design apparently the decisive factors.) Grand Central provides an interesting commentary on the semiotics of size since, when it was built, it was one of the largest buildings in the immediate area, and now its neighbors tower above it. Originally, size enhanced its importance directly, while today its size differential, like a dramatic pause in a speech, captures the attention and the imagination, and permits the station to retain and even heighten its aura of urban importance.○

□ The problem of size is one of the least subtle but most troublesome confronting contemporary urban design. As buildings get bigger, they become increasingly like dinosaurs, with the ability to inflict tremendous accidental damage with one flick of a poorly designed tail. The mannered tops of several recent buildings, notably Citicorp○and AT&T (550-568 Madison Avenue),○would have escaped notice on smaller buildings, but their massive size gives them a visual prominence, and therefore a symbolic status, far out of proportion to their relative civic importance. Luckily, this is one problem that is largely self-correcting. The tall buildings that have become the symbols of one era tend periodically to be demolished or dwarfed by a new set. And in the case of contemporary mid-Manhattan, there are so many new towers in the works that ultimately they are likely to cancel each other out.

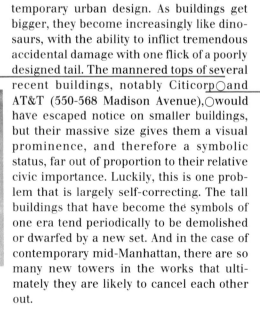

□ The concept of size includes mass, or volume, as well as height, but mass alone has rarely been enough to generate a sense of urban importance. In New York, some of the buildings with the greatest amounts of floor space (for example, the Port Authority Building at 111 Eighth Avenue at 15th Street○and the Starret Lehigh Building at 601 W. 26th Street)○have remained anonymous, while several others that convey an impression of grandeur and huge volume are, like Grand Central, not really that big at all. This is the magic of scale, the basis of which, in an architectural or urban context, is the human figure.○ ○ The dimensions of a building, necessarily, must be determined by the needs of the people who are to use it: If a window or door is too big, it can be impossible to open; if a ceiling is too low, people hit their heads. As a result, certain dimensions and proportions are "normal" and deviations are noteworthy; an unusually low ceiling can be either oppressive or cozy, while a high one can seem grand or sterile. But whether the effect is appealing or not, any appreciable deviation from the "normal" range of scale relationships is almost certain to have a theatrical effect.

□ Unfortunately, the impulse to use scale to emphasize a building's symbolic importance, even where it is appropriate, often goes beyond impressiveness and becomes intimidating. Sometimes this is intentional;○often it is not,○as in the Family Court building at 60 Lafayette Street. It is the rare building which manages to strike a balance between awe and comfort, and which, like any effective art, makes the viewer feel larger than life rather than smaller. This is accomplished by establishing a dual frame of reference, usually one at eye level and the other above, roughly corresponding to the view from close up and the view from farther away. From a distance, the broad features of a facade are within the normal angle of vision, and exaggerations of scale can be felt, although softened somewhat by the intervening space.○,○As the viewer approaches, the overscale elements loom overhead as the smaller, eye-level details assume greater importance. Sometimes these details can be purely architectural – moldings, column bases, light brackets, stonework, and the like – producing a formal, monumental effect,○or they can be functional – driveways, doors, stores, telephones, water fountains, and so on.○By utilizing both formal and functional devices, Grand Central succeeds admirably in permitting the public to feel the building's drama and importance without being made to feel insignificant.

□ Scale, too, has been a casualty of both new technologies and new architectural styles. The curtain wall, particularly, made it possible to eliminate all of the normal visual events (i.e., doors and windows) from building facades, and the design community

Ornament

seized the opportunity. The result has been buildings with no points of reference, no visible relationship to the size of the viewer, and therefore no scale at all, as in the World Trade Center,○or the Ford Foundation at 320 E. 43rd Street.○Inevitably lost as well has been the sense of dual perspective for the viewer approaching a building, since both functional and architectural detail have been as staunchly avoided at eye level as in the upper reaches of the facade. In fact, we have seen a perverse reversal of the old principles, with buildings whose exaggerated entrances face narrow streets where they can never be seen from a distance, and which become inexorably more featureless (and ominous) as they are approached. ○ Happily, there are also a few new buildings which have successfully used scale as a humanizing tool instead of for simplistic theatrics,○as at 767 Third Avenue.

□ The final medium for the expression of myth is ornament. Although a building can be covered with ornament without evoking any strong symbolic resonances○(Alwyn Court, 180 W. 58th Street), a single ornamental feature is sometimes enough to provide a dramatic focus for a building, a neighborhood, or even an entire city. ○And Grand Central uses this device as effectively as all the others. There is large ornament○,○and small corresponding to, and reinforcing, the alternations between grand and human scale. This is one area, however, where Grand Central may prove to be just a museum piece, and not a model for the future. Ornament has become so totally separate from architecture○,○(World Trade Center Plaza, and the sculpture in front of the McGraw-Hill Building at 1221 Sixth Avenue), and most attempts to reunite them have been so tentative and unconvincing○ that the whole concept appears to be either obsolete or, at least, in need of complete redefinition. Is mirror glass or the slanted top of Citicorp ornament? This is a problem in design metaphysics which Grand Central can do little, if anything, to illuminate.

127

□ It should be apparent by now that the mythic components of design have proved to be a new Pandora's box full of conceptual confusion and urban divisiveness. When every new building tries to grab the spotlight by cloaking itself in the historic trappings of civic status, the city becomes increasingly balkanized, its sense of cohesiveness erodes, and good buildings are trivialized by bad ones.

□ The response, however, should not be the suppression of myth, for that would just take us from chaos to sterility. Instead, we must relearn how to harness the symbols, the way it was done on the grandest scale by Grand Central and, at the other end of the spectrum, by the simplest brownstones and tenements.

□ Getting the symbols under control is not enough, however, unless at the same time we can tie individual buildings back to their environments – internal and external – and thereby begin to knit the city back together again.

□ Implementation, as usual, is the last and highest hurdle, and that is where Grand Central, and this exhibit, could play a useful role. In its relationships to the people who pass through and around it, Grand Central provides an ideal model for legislation that could begin to redefine the relationship between buildings and the city. Provisions might include:

1. Require that most buildings extend to the sidewalk – that is, eliminate plazas and other street-level setbacks. (Newly proposed zoning for midtown New York, and design guidelines for several other areas, have incorporated such a provision, which is actually just a return to pre-1961 New York City zoning practice.)

2. Require that a specified percent of sidewalk frontage be devoted to commercial and other active uses.

3. Require that a specified percent of the frontage on interior public spaces also be devoted to commercial and other active uses.

4. Require the provision of service facilities – seating, telephones, drinking fountains, waste receptacles, etc.

5. Require that basic civic functions be accommodated – subway entrances, bus stops, police/fire stations, etc.

6. Prohibit changes in the street grid – for example, plazas, pedestrian walks, parks, etc. – except by legislative action.

□ Despite its frequent over-use and misuse in the recent past, zoning would be a logical vehicle for such provisions, which could be incentive-based or mandatory. Tax and environmental legislation may also have roles to play, as they already do in the area of historic preservation. And such regulations would naturally have to be tailored to local needs (in some climates it might be desirable to encourage arcaded or even fully enclosed sidewalks, for example), and would have to tread very lightly to avoid the monotony and lifelessness which zoning has often produced. What is needed is a set of very broad guidelines establishing priorities in a city-wide context, not a detailed set of rules.

□ The best we can hope for from such guidelines is a redirection of the functional aspects of urban design – a redefinition of the relationship between a building, inside and out, and its users. The mythic/conceptual roles that buildings play are far too fragile to survive direction by even the most carefully drafted legislation. The closest we can come is the legal protection of existing good buildings and neighborhoods, but legislating in the province of symbolism for new buildings can only produce architecture which, at best, echoes the banalities of socialist official-style, and at worst, drifts toward the excesses of the fascists.

□ The fact that our ability to legislate urban change is sharply limited with regard to function and nonexistent when it comes to symbolism does not, however, leave us as powerless as it might seem. There is one option remaining which, though untested, has fascinating and apparently limitless potential: raising the level of mass public design awareness. Once people begin to see, through exhibits like this and buildings like Grand Central, what makes a building or a city work and how it can directly benefit them, they will begin to demand quality, to ridicule – as the design professionals have failed to do – mediocrity, and to reject failures. The design of our cities could become a matter not just for a small group of city planners and architects, but a national issue, alongside "save the whales" and "stop nuclear power." It is, after all, an environmental issue, directly affecting that large majority of the population which lives or works in cities.

□ The powers of zoning, in fact, are nothing compared to the effect people could have on design if, say, a new corporate headquarters building became the target of a Johnny Carson monologue, or if architect jokes replaced ethnic jokes, or if teachers brought their classes on field trips to Grand Central instead of to the Museum.

David Bonderman

THE GRAND CENTRAL TERMINAL LITIGATION AND THE DEVELOPMENT OF PRESERVATION LAW

Schemes for the proposed 55 – story office tower over Grand Central, 1968, 1969.
Architects: Marcel Breuer & Associates.

■ Grand Central Terminal was opened to the public in 1913 and immediately attracted international acclaim, not only because of the imaginative architectural solution to the difficult engineering problem posed by having to construct the station over underground tracks, but because of the building's massive scale and the beauty of its architectural design. Commentators at the time particularly admired the fine Beaux-Arts exterior, the sculptured details, and the imposing statues of Mercury, Hercules, and Minerva atop the 42nd Street facade. In time, as one of the courts in the 1970s litigation over the terminal would find, Grand Central came to occupy a special place in the architecture of New York City:

Grand Central Terminal is an important and irreplaceable component of the special uniqueness of New York City's best known buildings. Along with the Empire State Building and the Statue of Liberty, the image of its facade symbolizes New York City for millions of visitors and residents. [1]

□ Because of its unique importance to the architectural and cultural history of New York City, in 1967 the terminal became one of the first buildings the city Landmarks Preservation Commission designated as a landmark – that is, a building legally entitled to special protection against alteration or demolition. This designation and its subsequent impact on the plans of the Penn Central Transportation Company, the terminal's owner, to build a modern fifty-five-story tower on top of the terminal, led to major litigation. The Penn Central and allied real estate interests were arrayed on one side; on the other were preservationists and concerned members of the general public. The resulting 1978 decision of the United States Supreme Court not only saved Grand Central Terminal from substantial alteration or worse, but as legal precedent will have an important impact on other landmarks and historic buildings and districts throughout the country.

□ This essay is designed to provide a brief history and introduction to the development of preservation laws, to discuss the legal and philosophical bases of these laws, and to describe in some detail the issues raised and decided by the Supreme Court's decision in the Grand Central Terminal litigation, *Penn Central Transportation Co.* v. *City of New York.* [2]

The beginnings of preservation law.
□ In the first hundred or so years of the United States, the general suspicion of government led the framers of the Constitution to include the Fifth Amendment (protecting private ownership of property) and the now seldom-recalled Tenth Amendment (that all powers not specifically enumerated in the Constitution are reserved to the states or to the people) in the Bill of Rights and led to similar provisions in many state constitutions. The same suspicion ensured that anything that might be construed as governmental intrusion on use of private property was narrowly limited by the courts.

□ The limited governmental authority over privately owned real estate was based upon two legal principles. First the government could force an owner to sell his property where the property was needed by the government for a "public purpose," known as the power of eminent domain. Second, if it could be shown that it was necessary to preserve the health and welfare of the citizenry, the government could regulate private property under what is known as the "police power." Both the public purpose and police power doctrines were interpreted narrowly. As a result, regulation was generally limited to prevention of crime, fire, illness, and similar direct disasters.

□ In such a legal climate, there was little concern either with land-use regulation in general or with the preservation of particular buildings and structures. Not until after the Civil War, and reaching its height from about 1890 to 1930, did the situation change significantly.

Some early aspects of preservation.
□ The change began with the growing popular recognition that reminders of a common past helped maintain the cultural unity of the country. [3] Nineteenth-century preservation activities ranged from the private fundraising efforts that led to the acquisition and preservation of George Washington's plantation at Mount Vernon in 1859 by the Mount Vernon Ladies' Association, [4] to the decision some years later by Congress to acquire a number of Civil War battlefield sites as memorials. Congress' decision, in turn, gave rise to the first significant preservation-related litigation. *United States* v. *Gettysburg Electric Railway Co.,* [5] decided by the Supreme Court in 1896, involved the condemnation of private property for the creation of a national battlefield memorial at Gettysburg. At that time, the idea that the government might, even by purchase, be involved in the preservation of historic sites was new and strange. In fact, the railway claimed that the condemnation was not for any public purpose as that principle was understood in constitutional law and, accordingly, was beyond the power of the federal government.

□ Ultimately, the Supreme Court concluded that the preservation of an important monument to the country's past was indeed a proper public purpose, on the ground that the history the battle represented "is rendered plainer and more durable by the fact that the Government of the United States, through its representatives in Congress assembled, abides and endeavors to perpetuate it by this most suitable recognition." Here then, for the first time, the Supreme Court recognized that preservation of a historic site was within the government's power, at least where the government purchased the property. Not considered, of course, was whether or to what extent the government might achieve a similar result by regulation.

The expansion of regulatory powers.
□ As America became more urban and as new architectural and building techniques allowed the construction of ever more massive buildings, cities and towns became concerned about retaining their character, particularly in residential neighborhoods. Local governments began to experiment with land-use controls on a broad scale. It had, of course, been accepted in the common law since medieval times that government regulatory powers were sufficient to control certain noxious uses such as slaughter houses, tanneries, gunpowder manufacturers, and the like. But early in the twentieth century, the Supreme Court decided a number of cases which extended the government's power to regulate land ownership. In the two most important decisions, *Welch* v. *Swasey,* decided in 1909, and *Village of Euclid* v. *Ambler Realty Co.,* decided in 1926, the Supreme Court decided, respectively, that the City of Boston could exercise its regulatory power to limit the height of buildings and that a comprehensive zoning ordinance adopted by a Cleveland suburb was constitutional. [6] Prior to the Supreme Court's rulings, about half the state courts had held that zoning laws were an unconstitutional interference with private property.

□ Of particular importance for our perspective with regard to landmark laws were the grounds for these two Supreme Court decisions. In both cases – and in a number of similar cases in the first thirty years of this century – the Supreme Court based its decision in large part on economic grounds. That is, the Court upheld the height restrictions in *Welch* and the zoning ordinance in *Euclid* on the ground that the government was properly using its police powers to protect and enhance property values, and that the purpose of the restrictions was, therefore, economic.

While these cases represented an expansion of the states' police powers beyond the hard-core health and safety issues to which that power had previously been limited, they did not authorize regulation for aesthetic purposes alone. Indeed, in both cases the opponents of the ordinances involved contended, with some success in the lower courts, that the ordinances were unconstitutional because their true motivation was to protect aesthetics. This argument did not prevail, not because the principle was held incorrect, but because the Supreme Court found an economic basis for the legislative action. Thus, an important question remained as to whether the government could regulate essentially for aesthetic purposes.

In addition, each of these cases involved what lawyers call a "taking" claim. The Fifth Amendment of the Constitution, which applies to the federal government directly and to state and local governments through the Fourteenth Amendment, provides that property shall not be "taken" by the government without the payment of "just compensation."

In practical terms, this means that if the government elects to build a highway through your house, it may use its power of eminent domain to do so, but must pay you the fair market value of the house. While the framers of the Constitution apparently understood this taking clause to refer to eminent domain proceedings only, in the latter part of the nineteenth century and early part of the twentieth century the courts began to apply the taking clause to government regulation, particularly but not exclusively to land-use regulation. As Supreme Court Justice Oliver Wendell Holmes said in a famous 1922 decision:

The general rule at least is that while property may be regulated to a certain extent, if regulation goes too far, it will be recognized as a taking.[7]

What Holmes apparently meant was that the government was free to regulate property for appropriate reasons without making payment, but that if the burden imposed on a landowner by the regulations was too great in an economic sense (whatever that might mean in a particular case), then the regulation would either be struck down or payment would be required.

In rejecting claims that the Boston height and Euclid zoning ordinances were a taking, the Supreme Court found that the effects (there was evidence that the Euclid ordinance lowered the value of commercial property which was rezoned to residential use by nearly 90 percent) were not too severe. The Court reached this result because it concluded that the so-called mutuality of the benefits and burdens imposed by these ordinances made them fair to the owners.

Put simply, the Court held that the burden imposed on a property owner by limiting the height of his building was permissible without compensation because the same burden was imposed on all other nearby property owners, and because at the same time the benefits – better light, less crowding, and so forth – of the height limitation (which, as noted, were treated in largely economic terms) also applied to all property owners. Thus, the burden was considered to be non-discriminatory.

This was the background under which preservation laws later developed.

The historic district ordinances.

The earliest preservation laws, passed in the 1930s, dealt with what are today known as historic districts. These laws sought to protect a relatively few well-known neighborhoods or districts whose historic and architectural character was of national or international reknown, by limiting demolition and alterations of historic buildings and imposing architectural controls on construction. The first three such ordinances were passed in Charleston in 1931, covering the antebellum section of the city; in New Orleans in 1937, covering the Vieux Carré (French Quarter); and in San Antonio in 1939.[8] By 1955 there were twenty such ordinances, by 1965 there were 100 of them, and by 1975 there were approximately 500 historic district ordinances in the United States. They featured several common philosophical underpinnings and several common characteristics.

First, perhaps as much because of the decisions of the Supreme Court discussed earlier as because of the general perceptions of the time, a common stated rationale for the ordinances was to preserve for economic reasons the historic character of the districts involved, specifically to encourage and preserve the tourist industry. Although many of the statutes and ordinances referred to historic and architectural considerations, these factors were rarely used as the legal basis for the legislation.

Second, each of the statutes functioned in a fashion similar to the zoning ordinances that had previously been approved by the Supreme Court. That is, they applied not to a single structure, but to an entire area, and thus they were consistent with the notion of mutuality of burden and benefit.

Third, each of these ordinances represented a major practical advance in the sense that each imposed tight architectural controls, in some instances requiring owners to adequately maintain their property, and each significantly limited an owner's ability to alter or demolish his private property. This latter aspect of the ordinances proved controversial, but each was sustained, even by relatively conservative state courts, under the zoning analysis previously discussed.[9]

The reader will note, however, that the historic district ordinances and the cases discussed so far leave open a number of important questions. What, for example, is the validity of a regulation that openly depends upon aesthetics as its justification? What restrictions are permissible where the preservation-oriented statute applies to a single building or structure, such as Grand Central Terminal, rather than to an entire district? And how great a limitation would the Court sustain on an owner's intended use of his property? These questions remained for the *Penn Central* litigation to confront in 1978.

The New York City landmarks law.

The same growth of historical awareness that led to the pressure for national battlefield monuments and the protection of historic districts in Charleston, New Orleans, and elsewhere led ultimately to a heightened national consciousness about the importance of individual buildings and structures of great merit. Many of the historic buildings initially considered as worthy of preservation were then in the hands of the federal, state, or local governments. But others, of which Grand Central Terminal is a leading example, were privately owned. In 1956 New York became the first state to authorize its municipalities to enact "landmark" ordinances designed to protect individual buildings, as opposed to historic districts. And in 1965 New York City became the first major city to pass a landmark ordinance with any significant protection for designated individual buildings.

In enacting the landmark ordinance, the City Council determined that

the protection, enhancement, perpetuation and use of improvements and landscape features of special character or special historical or aesthetic interest or value is a public necessity and is required in the interest of the health, prosperity, safety and welfare of the people.[10]

□ Accordingly, the city established a statutory plan pursuant to which a Landmarks Preservation Commission was created and empowered, after a public hearing, to designate qualifying structures of significant historic or aesthetic merit as landmarks. (The commission was also empowered to designate qualifying areas and neighborhoods as historic districts.) The next step in the process is that the impact of the designation on other city land-use regulations then becomes the subject of a report by the city Planning Commission, and the designation is submitted for approval by the Board of Estimate.[11] Once a property is designated, construction, reconstruction, alteration, and demolition are regulated by the Landmarks Preservation Commission. A proposed modification of a designated property will not be allowed unless the commission finds that it will have no effect on the protected architectural features, is otherwise consistent with the purposes of the landmarks law, or is required to avoid economic hardship to the owner. In addition, a section of the New York zoning resolutions (which have the force of law) allows a property owner to "transfer" unused "development rights" – called TDRs – from a landmark to other nearby property under certain restrictions.[12] (New York is virtually alone in adopting TDRs, a measure no other major city has found necessary.)

Grand Central Terminal as a landmark.

□ Acting pursuant to the landmarks law, the New York City Landmarks Preservation Commission has designated to date nearly 600 individual buildings and structures as landmarks, along with forty-one historic districts, twenty-five interior landmarks, and eight scenic landmarks. One of the first landmark designations, and one of the most important, was Grand Central Terminal. After several public hearings, on August 2, 1967, the Landmarks Preservation Commission issued the designation,[13] and on September 21, 1967, the designation was confirmed by the Board of Estimate as required by the landmark law. The Penn Central Transportation Company, as owner of the terminal, opposed the designation, but did not appeal from it. Accordingly, the designation became final, and Grand Central Terminal was subject to the protections of the New York landmark law.

□ In 1968, Penn Central and some of its subsidiaries entered into a lease with UGP Properties, Inc., a subsidiary of a British company. UGP proposed to construct a fifty-five-story office building atop the terminal. To carry out this scheme, UGP and Penn Central hired the internationally famous architect Marcel Breuer. Breuer proposed two alternate plans, which became known as Breuer I and Breuer II Revised. Both schemes would have placed a tower approximately 500 feet high on the top of the terminal and required the destruction of a portion of the interior concourse. The Breuer II Revised plan also would have required the actual demolition of the terminal's 42nd Street facade. Both plans would have meant the end of Grand Central Terminal in its present form and would have radically altered the imagery of Park Avenue.

□ In accordance with the New York landmark law, Penn Central and UGP filed applications with the Landmarks Preservation Commission requesting a certificate either that the proposed construction and demolition would have no effect on the protected architectural features of the terminal's exterior or that any effect produced would be "appropriate." Two sets of hearings were held on the proposals. Those in favor of the Breuer plans included not only the architect, the developer, and the New York Real Estate Board, but also the administrator for architecture and planning of the Metropolitan Museum of Art. Those opposed included Mayor (then Congressman) Edward Koch, the American Institute of Architects, The Municipal Art Society, the president of the City Council, and leading preservationists and citizens at large. An enormous public clamor ensued.

□ On August 26, 1969, the Commission denied the Penn Central/UGP applications on the ground that the proposed tower and demolitions would "affect and change the exterior architectural features" and that those changes would be highly inappropriate.[14] According to the Commission,

to balance a fifty-five-story office tower above a flamboyant Beaux-Arts facade seems nothing more than an aesthetic joke. . . . The "addition" would be four times as high as the existing structure and would reduce the landmark itself to the status of a curiosity.

□ The Commission went on to say that approving the demolition of a major portion of the terminal as proposed by Penn Central and UGP

would be in flagrant violation of the Commission's responsibility. To protect a landmark, one does not tear it down. To perpetuate its architectural features one does not strip them off. . . . To approve the Breuer proposal would mean the loss not only of one more fine building, in addition to the many that were lost before there was a landmark law to protect them, it would mean the loss of an officially designated landmark and one that "evokes a spirit that is unique in this City."

The Landmarks Preservation Commission thus rejected both of the Penn Central/Breuer proposals, and the stage for court litigation was set.

The *Penn Central* litigation in the lower courts.

□ On October 7, 1969, shortly after receiving the decision of the Landmarks Commission, Penn Central filed a lawsuit against the city in the Supreme Court of the State of New York. (Despite its name, New York's Supreme Court is the state's trial or lowest court.) Penn Central's complaint made a number of assertions, including that whether the terminal should be a landmark at all was "highly debatable and at best doubtful," and that the two Breuer proposals were "widely acclaimed" and "truly appropriate." Such allegations were not, however, the heart of the case, because questions regarding architectural appropriateness and the worthiness of the landmark designation were not really an issue.

□ At the heart of Penn Central's lawsuit were two claims. The first was that the effect of the commission's denial of the building permit was so burdensome as to amount to a "taking" of Penn Central's property without just compensation. The second was that the effect of the landmark ordinance was to unconstitutionally discriminate against Penn Central because by designating the terminal a landmark the City of New York had required Penn Central to bear burdens not required of other nearby landowners. In other words, Penn Central was claiming that there was no mutuality of benefits and burdens. In addition, although the company did not explicitly raise it, the *Penn Central* litigation posed an underlying question regarding the validity of the New York landmark law, since it had been enacted on the basis of aesthetic reasons. The City of New York, of course, denied each of the relevant allegations and the matter eventually went to trial before Irving Saypol, a trial court judge in the New York Supreme Court, sitting in Manhattan.

□ During the trial, Penn Central's major effort was directed to the taking issue. Accordingly, the company introduced evidence attempting to show that it had been operating Grand Central Terminal at a loss of nearly $2 million a year for some years and that it could not earn a reasonable return on its property in the current circumstances. The company also introduced its agreement with

UGP Properties, pursuant to which Penn Central was to receive $1 million rent per year during construction of the proposed tower and $3 million a year for fifty years thereafter. Thus, according to Penn Central, denial of the certificate to construct the Breuer tower effectively precluded it from earning large sums and prevented it from operating its property at a profit.

□ The trial judge, who was apparently not a fan of the terminal ("It leaves no reaction here other than of long neglected faded beauty"), write a short opinion which was filed on January 21, 1975.[15] The opinion does not contain any substantial discussion of the important legal principles involved, but Judge Saypol did find that Penn Central had adequately shown such economic hardship as to establish that the landmark restrictions were an unconstitutional taking of its property. The judge issued an order holding that the designation of the terminal, and the subsequent restrictions, was unconstitutional. This order, if upheld, would have allowed Penn Central to build either of the Breuer schemes or, for that matter, to demolish the terminal entirely.

□ In the State of New York, however, the trial court is only the first in a three-tiered system that includes two appellate courts: The intermediate court is known as the Appellate Division, and the highest court of the state is called the Court of Appeals. In the normal course, a litigant who is dissatisfied with the result of a trial court may appeal to the Appellate Division. Thereafter, if one of the parties is still not satisfied, he may appeal to the Court of Appeals.

□ In this instance, the City of New York took the trial judge's decision to the Appellate Division, and on December 16, 1975, the city won a three-to-two decision, reversing the trial court and upholding the decision of the Landmarks Preservation Commission.[16] The three-judge majority of the Appellate Division found that the trial court had incorrectly analyzed the facts and misapplied the law.

□ Specifically, the Appellate Division found that Penn Central's claims that it was losing several million dollars a year operating Grand Central Terminal had not been substantiated. The court pointed out that in making those claims, Penn Central had allocated many of its costs for running the railway (for example, maintaining a station master and railroad information clerks, maintaining and cleaning the railway portions of the terminal, and so on) to the terminal operation instead of to the railway business, and that Penn Central allowed the railway to use the terminal rent free. In addition, the court noted that Penn Central had not proved that any losses it did incur were necessary or could not have been prevented by better management or more efficient use of the available rental space.

□ On the taking question, the court concluded that the relevant issue was whether the restrictions imposed by the Landmarks Commission deprived Penn Central of "all reasonable use" of its property. The majority held that Penn Central had not met that burden because it could and did operate the terminal as a railway station.

□ Penn Central went on to appeal the decision to the highest court of the state, the New York Court of Appeals. On June 23, 1977, its seven judges unanimously upheld the Appellate Division, and concluded that the landmark restrictions were permissible.[17] The Court of Appeals decided that, with respect to the taking question, only the effect upon "the privately created ingredient" needed to be considered. By this, the court apparently meant to separate out the value attributable to (a) the location or other such attributes of the property that derived from the result of public expenditures from (b) the value attributable to the owner's private effort, and look only at the effect on the latter. No other court has ever used such a test – which, if one considers it, is practically impossible to administer: How, for example, would one value Grand Central Terminal if it were in Des Moines instead of on Park Avenue? Moreover, that test was not obviously consistent with the legal doctrines previously discussed which had emerged to date from the U.S. Supreme Court.

□ After it had exhausted the appeal process in the New York courts, Penn Central sought review by the Supreme Court of the United States. Such review is discretionary with the Supreme Court, which accepts less than 1 percent of the cases brought to it. Perhaps because of the unique opinion by the New York Court of Appeals, the Supreme Court agreed to hear the Penn Central case. As a result, the Grand Central Terminal dispute became the first land-use regulation case of any sort to reach the Court in two decades and the first, and to date only, such case to consider the merits of landmark preservation.

The Supreme Court decision in *Penn Central.*

□ In the Supreme Court, Penn Central made arguments which, although refined in certain respects, were not dissimilar from those it made in the lower courts. Thus, the company's major claim was that rejecting the permit to build the Breuer tower atop Grand Central was an unconstitutional taking of its property because the rejection completely denied it the use of the air rights over the terminal. Penn Central also claimed that the landmark designation was unconstitutionally discriminatory in that it singled out one property for special unfavorable treatment.

□ In view of the importance of the case, briefs were filed not only by the parties, but by a variety of other governmental units and private groups whose interests might have been affected by the Court's decision. Thus, for example, the Pacific Legal Foundation – an organization whose conservative philosophy resembles that of now-Secretary of the Interior James Watt's Mountain States Legal Foundation – and the New York Real Estate Board filed briefs in support of Penn Central. On the other hand, the Solicitor General of the United States, the states of New York and California, the Committee to Save Grand Central Station – a group of New York City civic associations and prominent individuals – the National Trust for Historic Preservation, the Municipal Art Society, the cities of New Orleans, Boston, and San Antonio, and a number of other conservation and preservation groups filed briefs in support of New York City.

□ In an opinion that was a major victory for the future of Grand Central Terminal, and significantly promotes historic preservation everywhere,[18] on June 26, 1978, Justice William J. Brennan, writing for a six-justice majority, upheld the action of the New York City Landmarks Preservation Commission.

□ First, the Court laid to rest the notion that aesthetic considerations alone are not a valid basis for the use of the government's police power, explicitly noting "that states and cities may enact land-use restrictions or controls to enhance the quality of life by preserving the character and desirable aesthetic features of a City. . . ."[19]

□ Second, in rejecting the Penn Central taking claim, the decision in *Penn Central Transportation Co.* v. *City of New York* makes it clear that historic preservation qualifies as just another form of land-use regulation as far as the law is concerned. Justice Brennan's decision accomplishes this by applying the same concepts that have been used in the zoning cases starting at the turn of the century, as described earlier. As a result (although, as we shall see, the Court did not entirely resolve the issue) based on a series of subsequent lower court decisions, it is now reasonable to conclude that to show successfully a taking in a preservation case a landowner will have to demonstrate that retaining the historic structure will deny him all reasonable economic use of the property.[20]

□ Perhaps the most significant new factor to emerge from the *Penn Central* case is that it is now plain that protection can be given to individual landmarks as well as to historic districts. The Court explicitly rejected the claim that designating individual landmarks is discriminatory and, therefore, improper, at least where a city has designated a substantial number of landmarks.

□ But because *Penn Central* involves factual circumstances which may be unusual, the effect of the decision is not entirely clear on some frequently litigated issues. The New York courts had found as a matter of fact that the restrictions resulting from Grand Central's landmark designation did not prevent Penn Central from continuing to use the terminal as a railway station and to earn a reasonable return along the lines it had always done. No one knows, for example, what the result would have been had the factual findings in the New York Court of Appeals and the lower courts been different. What happens, for instance, if the owner can show that his return is only 1 percent or 2 percent, or that he has no return?

□ In addition, as mentioned earlier, New York City has an unusual transfer of development rights – or TDR – program, which allows an owner to move unused development rights from one site to another. There was a strong argument by Penn Central that these TDRs were not very valuable or, at least, were not as valuable as the fifty-five-story office tower that the city rejected. Everyone conceded, however, that the TDRs had some value. As a result, while many observers thought that Penn Central's taking claims were very weak as a factual matter, others have suggested that the outcome might have been different if there had been no TDRs. I do not think so.

□ What can we say about the effect of *Penn Central* in the short term? Certainly by upholding New York City's denial of a permit to build the Breuer tower, the decision saved Grand Central Terminal. Furthermore, the Supreme Court's decision in *Penn Central* avoided what would have been a national architectural and planning disaster had the case been decided otherwise. Considering the other necessary social services in financially hard-pressed cities, no historic preservation program can realistically expect sufficient municipal funds to buy important buildings and sites, or their air rights, from major developers. Accordingly, if the Court had accepted Penn Central's argument that it had to be paid the full value of its lost air rights because the landmark restriction had prevented desired development, meaningful landmark programs would have been extremely difficult to establish. So after *Penn Central*, landmark programs can go forward, and the case has provided an impetus for the passage of stronger preservation statutes throughout the country.

□ The long-term implications of the *Penn Central* decision are not as clear, either for the terminal itself or for the future of preservation law. It is noteworthy that the Supreme Court in *Penn Central* did not hold that Grand Central Terminal could never be demolished or that the effect of the landmark ordinance as applied to the terminal could never be held unconstitutional. Rather, the Court held only that on the facts that Penn Central was able to prove, the landmark ordinance was constitutional and must be enforced. In theory, this leaves Penn Central free to come back at some later point to try to prove the case that it failed to prove this time. But the practicalities are that Penn Central most likely will never be able to prove the facts it needs to show a taking.

□ With respect to landmark law and historic preservation generally, the court decisions since *Penn Central* have tended to be quite favorable to preservation and environmental interests. The Supreme Court has heard two land-use cases in the three years since *Penn Central*, and, while neither of them was decided on the merits, the decisions in both contain language helpful to the cause of preservation. For example, in *Agins* v. *City of Tiburon*,[21] the Court observed that a taking occurs only where a restriction "denies an owner economically viable use of his land." And in the *San Diego Gas & Electric* case,[22] a number of justices made this same observation. In addition, the lower federal and state courts, perhaps taking their cues from *Penn Central*, have generally been very strong in upholding preservation ordinances.

□ Those who support preservation efforts can take comfort, then, from the general trend in the decisional law. Those who oppose them point out that, in the broadest sense, these decisions are political, and that, just as in the earlier part of this century the courts began to significantly expand permissible government regulation, now with widespread antipathy to government regulation there may be the prospect that courts will begin to moderate their views and move the other way. Whatever happens, however, it is a reasonable bet that the statues of Mercury, Hercules, and Minerva on Grand Central Terminal's 42nd Street facade will look down on Park Avenue for a long time to come.

1. The quote is from Finding of Fact No. 3 in the Order of the Appellate Division in the New York Supreme Court, filed April 7, 1976. The decision of the Appellate Division is reported at 50 A.D.2d 265, 377 N.Y.S.2d 20 (1975), but the findings of fact are not reprinted there.
2. 438 U.S. 104 (1978).
3. A good discussion of these historical aspects of preservation is contained in C.M. Rose, "Preservation and Community: New Directions in the Law of Historic Preservation," 33 Stanford Law Review 473 (1981).
4. An interesting description of the long and ultimately successful struggle to preserve Mount Vernon appears in C. B. Hosmer, **The Presence of the Past**, pp. 41-57 (1965).
5. 160 U.S. 668 (1896).
6. The two cases are reported at 214 U.S. 91 (1909) and 272 U.S. 365 (1926), respectively.
7. **Pennsylvania Coal Co.** v. **Mahon**, 260 U.S. 393, 415 (1922).
8. The early ordinances are discussed in some detail in J. Morrison, **Historic Preservation Law** (2d ed. 1965).
9. E.g., **City of New Orleans** v. **Inpastato**, 198 La. 206, 3 So. 2d 559 (1941) (upholding New Orleans Vieux Carré ordinance); **City of Sante Fe** v. **Gamble Skogmo, Inc.**, 73 N.M. 410, 389 P.2d 13 (1964) (upholding Santa Fe historic district ordinance).
10. N.Y.C. Administrative Code Section 205-1.0b.
11. The Board of Estimate is made up of the Mayor (Chairman), the Controller, the President of the City Council, and the five borough presidents.
12. The landmark ordinance is contained in N.Y.C. Charter, Section 534, and N.Y.C. Administrative Code Sections 205-1.0/207-21.0. The transfer of development rights regulations are contained in the New York City Zoning Resolutions, Sections 74-79/793.
13. Landmarks Preservation Commission Decision No. LPC 0266.
14. Landmarks Preservation Commission Decision Nos. LPC 69005, 69006.
15. The lower court decision is not reported.
16. The Appellate Division decision appears at 50 A.D.2d 265, 377 N.Y.S.2d 20 (1975).
17. The Court of Appeals decision is reported at 42 N.Y.2d 324, 397 N.Y.S.2d 914, 366 N.E.2d 1271 (1977).
18. The Supreme Court decision is reported at 438 U.S. 104 (1978).
19. 438 U.S. at 129. In **City of New Orleans** v. **Dukes**, 427 U.S. 297, 304 (1976), which upheld a New Orleans ordinance barring most pushcart vendors from the historic French Quarter, the court intimated that aesthetic considerations were a valid basis for police power regulation but did not explicitly so hold. The **Penn Central** holding has now been followed by most states.
20. E.g. **Maher** v. **City of New Orleans**, 516 F.2d 1051 (5th Cir. 1975); **William C. Haas & Co.** v. **City and County of San Francisco**, 605 F.2d 1117 (9th Cir. 1979); **900 E Street Associates** v. **Department of Housing and Community Development**, 430 A.2d 1387 (D.C. App. 1981).
21. **Agins** v. **City of Tiburon**, 447 U.S. 255, 260 (1980).
22. **San Diego Gas & Electric Co.** v. **City of San Diego**, 101 S. Ct. 1287, 1301 (1981) (Brennan, J., dissenting).

Note: In addition to the cases cited in the notes, the following publications contain interesting expositions of either the historical basis or the legal issues surrounding preservation:

D. Bonderman, "Constitutional Issues for Preservation Law," 1 **Legal Notes and Viewpoints** 109 (1981).
F. Bosselman, **The Taking Issue** (1973).
Fitch and Waite, **Grand Central Terminal and Rockefeller Center: Historical Critical Estimate of Their Significance** (1974).
C. B. Hosmer, **The Presence of the Past** (1965).
J. Jacobs, **The Death and Life of Great American Cities** (1961).
J. Morrison, **Historic Preservation Law** (2d ed. 1965).
C. M. Rose, "Preservation and Community: New Directions in the Law of Historic Preservation," 33 **Stanford Law Review** 473 (1981).
N. Weinberg, **Historic Preservation in American Towns and Cities** (1979).

Hugh Hardy

Park Avenue ramp, west side of terminal, March 1982.

■ Great urban centers are distinguished by their density, diversity, and ease of access. For almost seventy years Grand Central Terminal has represented a brilliant synthesis of all three. Its multileveled mix of activities, central location, clear and easy circulation – all combined in heroic celebration of public gathering – have long been a hallmark of urban design. Yet these past triumphs are also the very cause of changes in the bones of this complex structure, changes which threaten both its present and future value.

□ Can we assume that Grand Central is safe? Does its landmark status ensure its survival as a viable public monument into a new century, now less than twenty years away? Will Grand Central be able to maintain its high rank in public esteem despite the dramatic changes that have taken place in ownership, operation, and constituency?

□ It is easy to become nostalgic about the great days of Grand Central. They belong to times more certain than our own, and represent an era that has surely passed, a time when private wealth was used to achieve public works built in the heart of the city. The romance about what was should not obscure the fact of the terminal's gradual dismemberment and physical decline – or our responsibility for acting now to ensure its future life and importance.

□ No longer two stations in one, nor blessed with 63 million passengers on 550 trains a day, Grand Central has become (with the exception of eleven Amtrak trains) merely one large train station servicing 500,000 pedestrians who use an unparalleled resource with all the ceremony of eating fast food. Bedecked with jarring commercial displays and third-class retail activities, its taxi ramps used for parking, its corridors made urinals, its platforms unwashed, and its roof in disrepair – this is not the stuff of urban grandeur.

□ To the unobservant, the terminal may appear unchanged, but instead of a multilayered transportation center surrounded by a diverse urban community, it is in danger of becoming a mass transit node set in an office park. Because Grand Central has been almost totally severed from the business of long-distance travel, the cachet of first-class life has deserted it for airports. While it remains urban in its remarkable density of use, it has lost much of the diversity of activities which characterized its early years. Department and clothing stores have departed its section of the city, where two major hotels are being converted for office use. Worse still, its access routes no longer match pedestrian flow.

Main concourse, March 1982.

136

Natural light, which helped generate the terminal's design, today is excluded from its skylights because of leaks, World War II blackout precautions, and current fiscal austerity. The six-story walls of glass, which once permitted startling views, are too grimy to offer more than shadows of the city beyond. The waiting room has become a limbo, stripped of its carved oak benches to discourage loitering, hacked up by new access routes at its eastern end, shorn of its connections to other levels along its south wall. Its original light-colored ceiling is stained dark brown, and its resplendent windows are rendered dimly translucent by dirt. It is a forlorn remnant of past magnificence now used to house a newsstand and a candy store.

It has been sly of time to leave the terminal's grand concourse, never designed for such things, as a repository for billboard displays, second only to Times Square in the mammoth scale of their commerical messages. These extravaganzas are not without charm. They offer public information, give stock news, and provide seasonal displays. They form part of the terminal's present architecture and contribute important revenues. And while outraged protests of aesthetic vandalism need to be balanced by economic reality, what would it be "worth" to stand in the grand concourse and see the Chrysler Building illuminated at night, or have sunlight stream through the terminal's south facade, replacing the commercial slogans and redundant clocks? If we are to allow such amenities to replace current necessities, we must establish a new economic strategy for the terminal's survival.

Like Central Park (conceived as a municipal benefit) or Rockefeller Center (conceived as enlightened commercialism), Grand Central combines eminent practicality with grand vision. In 1857 Frederick Law Olmsted's ideas of public betterment celebrated an uncompromising terrain by inventing a landscape. In 1932 John D. Rockefeller, left in the height of the Depression with the Metropolitan Opera's bad debit, created a symbol of commercial vitality out of an area of rooming houses. Grand Central joins two worlds to create an indoor park with an economic engine. Both still work, but they remain littered by disuse and misunderstanding.

This forty-eight-acre complex was blasted through 1.6 million cubic yards of the rock of Manhattan plus 1.2 million cubic yards of earth. It is a truly urban creation, now beset by a maze of multiple private and public ownerships which leaves the terminal and its connections no single spokesman. The full impact of these changes has been cushioned through a ninety-year lease (until 2062) with New York State's Metropolitan Transportation Authority (MTA), which operates a property still owned by Penn Central (now out of the railroad business and a successful real estate company). Under this lease to the Penn Central, the MTA has made several improvements. The terminal's main concourse has been cleaned and relit. A program to upgrade retail activities and improve signage has been initiated. The terminal is now closed from 1:30 a.m. to 5 a.m. to facilitate cleaning and prevent its household use by the homeless. Without these efforts by the MTA, Grand Central would clearly be suffering far greater neglect and disrepair.

Nonetheless, the eventual conflicts between mass access and symbolic grandeur will be resolved to the detriment of what we now see unless a coherent policy is established to benignly influence change.

As a decapitated Penn Station or the bowels of the World Trade Center amply illustrate, thousands of people per hour can be processed off and on commuter trains without the need for architectural amenities. The use of the terminal as nothing more than an elaborate series of corridors leading to commuter trains wastes a great resource.

The grand concourse and its interconnections form a series of great public spaces too precious to waste on routine and too expensive to maintain for such utilitarian needs alone. But how can this monument, which was built at the beginning of the twentieth century by private capital in the name of public welfare, best be operated in the rapidly approaching twenty-first century?

Decline and Renewal
The terminal's union of earth and sky, symbol and reality, necessity and amenity, is nowhere more apparent than in the grand concourse. Together with the south facade, these are the first elements that come to mind upon hearing the phrase "Grand Central." But what future use should be put to these heroic statements in steel and stone? Should the electric heavens be maintained for patrons of Off-Track Betting? Should the thousands of light bulbs that illuminate the cornice be renewed for 2,041 daily Amtrak passengers? Should the 10,000 panes of glass that enclose the concourse be washed for the benefit of students from Bridgeport? Can acres of marble be swept clean to enhance the journey of 500 people per day to Brewster, New York? The answers are as obvious as the question which lies within them. This is a room that belongs to everyone. But how to pay for it?

Architecturally, the terminal faces south. Its great ceremonial facade addresses a city whose center of gravity once lay below 42nd Street. Subsequent waves of construction engulfed the complex and now place midtown to the north. These shifts in population have led to significant changes in the terminal's pedestrian movement, the most notable being the added north connections through the Pan Am Building. In many ways current pedestrian flow is now backwards from the scheme's original concept. The circulation patterns once carefully designed to separate the terminal's different functions are now merged. Because commuter trains have come to dominate all levels, new access routes have been carved casually into original paths, and commercial space eats steadily into any potentially lucrative gaps.

The addition of escalators connecting the upper concourse directly to Park Avenue through the Pan Am Building has intensified commuter use of this level and short-circuited the ramp system designed to feed commuters into their originally separate stations on the lower level. If the MTA, which is wary of the increasing congestion, acts on proposals to add escalators between the upper and lower levels, the result will be still further changes in circulation patterns. These additions would pierce the grand concourse and void separations which ensured that long-distance passengers and baggage would flow through the upper level without unnecessary contact with the commuter trains below.

□ Other proposals currently in various stages of planning would further intensify the terminal's role in mass transit. For instance, connecting the Long Island Railroad to the terminal through an existing tunnel under the East River would dramatically increase commuter use. It is projected that the resulting increase in pedestrian traffic could then be channeled directly onto the tracks through a north-end access scheme. This would create subway-like sidewalk entrances from 45th to 48th streets and permit commuters to bypass the terminal altogether. Another suggested scheme would connect the railroad's Hudson division to Penn Station through freight yards on the west side, thus permitting all long-distance trains to completely bypass the terminal in favor of its pruned sister, Penn Station.

□ Assuming that the funding for implementing such ambitious plans becomes available, would the grand concourse survive as a great ceremonial public space? What complementary uses would best take advantage of its generous interior and enhance its economic viability? How can the terminal capitalize on the surrounding increase of office density? What services could its robust spaces provide for this new constituency?

□ Perhaps the most vexing issue in future considerations of the terminal is its relation to the subway. Why earlier plans to join commuter lines with the subway trains were abandoned is unknown. For some reason, the terminal's brilliant resolution of the conflicts between the needs of long-distance transportation and those of commuter travel did not extend to connections with the subways. Alas, a double set of looptracks makes a fifty-foot-tall curving wall, which inevitably prevents any direct connection. New linkages to the subway system are essential if the terminal is to succeed in the future as a regional transportation center.

□ Subways, once secure precincts of the middle class, have become synonymous with crime for many fearful would-be riders today. Nonetheless, because it is precisely the urban mix of diverse social groups which gives the terminal its character and vitality, the well-to-do also need to feel secure there. The carriage trade is as essential to the future of the terminal as all its commuters, shoppers, and tourists. Maintenance of so large a facility for the poor defies credulity. Making Grand Central simply a preserve for the rich cannot be justified. The terminal will work only if its density of use also accepts and encourages diversity.

□ Furthermore, New York City cannot afford the disintegration of subway service. It is the key to access for millions of people, and it must eventually be improved if the city is to survive as we know it. The subway is also a great New York institution, as inspiring of awe and wonder as the terminal itself. Assuming that it cannot be allowed to deteriorate further, we must see to it that its improvement yields ways to facilitate what are now incredibly cumbersome connections between the terminal and the IRT and Astoria subway trains. (Ironically, the Shuttle, that fragment of August Belmont's original rapid-mass-transit accomplishment with the most direct access from the terminal, is now under used.)

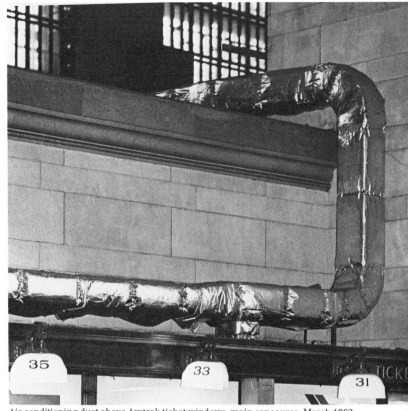

Air conditioning duct above Amtrak ticket windows, main concourse, March 1982.

Air conditioning unit at Conrail ticket windows, main concourse, March 1982.

Lexington Avenue IRT subway entrance, upper level, March 1982.

□ The other major issue in determining Grand Central's future – its expanded use by commuter traffic – portends an event that will only exacerbate congestion and require even more room for mass movements. Should capital funds become available to bring Long Island commuters directly to the terminal, even its vast reaches will be too small to shelter passengers in the event of malfunctions or accidents. It therefore seems wise to consider a secondary two-level commuter concourse built at the rail head. Its new access routes and vertical circulation could accommodate the intense twice-daily flow of passengers and their ticketing, retail, and service

needs. Construction of this concourse would make possible the new connections the MTA seeks between upper and lower levels, the platforms, and Park Avenue without destroying the architectural integrity of the grand concourse.

□ This is not to suggest that the grand public spaces of the terminal would be denied to commuter passengers, but rather that the necessary intensity of their rush-hour activities would not overwhelm its great ceremonial space.

□ The failure to resolve these difficult issues will inevitably lead to a lessening of value for the entire complex. But if the terminal's ease of movement can be ensured by creating its missing links to mass transit, its oft-praised virtues can then be extended into a new century.

□ The terminal has survived in public affection in part because it was *easy* to use. Circulation routes which make access difficult are against the grain. Since it is we who are now the custodians of its welfare, it is our responsibility to see to it that Grand Central will be perceived as valuable by a new generation whose aesthetic and cultural values may be radically different from our own.

An Economic Strategy

□ It does not seem alarmist to suggest that although the terminal is not in danger of being torn down, it is nonetheless being continually chewed on in ways which are damaging. But how do we act practically to guarantee that future generations will enjoy Grand Central's munificence?

□ To begin, the terminal must be perceived as more than just a very big railroad station. While its central purpose remains getting 180,000 people a day on and off trains, its location, architectural distinction, and multilevel connections with the city place it at the center of a unique marketplace. Grand Central offers an unmatched market for commercial uses *if* imaginative retail policies are followed as part of a coordinated program of improvement.

□ The idea that this complex could reassert itself as the Gateway to a Continent for rail transportation now seems unimaginable. Yet enough remains of heroic intent that it seems foolish to let the terminal suffer indifferent use, solely for the routine of commuting. It remains a gateway to the city, built in celebration of the romance of travel – and the economic might of the New York Central. If it is to continue to justify its splendor and remain economically viable, it must capitalize on its other legacy: a capacity to generate wealth.

□ The economic engine created by air-rights construction over its tracks was severed in 1970 by the bankruptcy of Penn Central. Subsequent sales have put all these railroad properties except the terminal itself into private ownership. Funding for the terminal's maintenance and operation now comes from a public body, the MTA. Despite its efforts to improve the terminal, the MTA is a regional transportation authority without experience in imaginative retail operations. Even Rockefeller Center, Inc., long distinguished by active promotion and skillful merchandising, has turned to outside professionals to consider the future of its commercial space. The Citicorp Center, a far more recent development, is intended to be a diverse urban showcase centered around the commodity of food, but its "market" is subsidized by Citicorp with the kind of resources that would be unimaginable for the MTA.

□ In considering the terminal's economic future, it is also instructive to compare Grand Central architecturally with the World Trade Center, operated by a public body, the Port Authority of New York and New Jersey. The design of its lower shopping concourse owes much to the precedent of Grand Central but at the World Trade Center, 204,000 square feet, covering 4.68 acres, are devoted to retail activities, while Grand Central offers only 2.66 acres. The World Trade Center passageways connect with surrounding streets and subways, but they lead to no common public space, no grand concourse. Even though the quality of retail activities is higher and more diverse than in Grand Central, the overall impression is that of a busy but dull basement.

□ When the terminal was operated as the showcase of a private corporation, it featured concerts and a variety of promotional events and seasonal displays. As we determine today to renew its vitality, it seems crucial for us to establish an imaginative overall policy for vigorous private-sector use of the terminal's public spaces. With the entrepreneurial skills available in New York, it would seem natural to use the terminal's central location and spacious architecture as a vehicle for a broad range of retail activities based upon the idea that New York is a national and international marketplace.

□ For this to succeed, it would be necessary to untangle rush-hour crowds from retail activities so the two would benefit, not conflict with one another. Charlie Brown's restaurant, for instance, certainly enjoys its location off the Pan Am lobby, as does the new bar located on the terminal's west balcony, but both are set apart from major circulation routes. (Charlie Brown's occupies the former baggage-handling area, and the bar's location once gave access to the long-distance baggage claim facility.)

□ A rigorous program would discover all kinds of "found" space in the terminal and yield many locations for prime retail activities which could be integrated into its circulation systems. Future development of these connections could contribute to a safer and more economically productive marketplace. Although spectacular linkages like the comparatively short-lived experiments with air connections to airports are unlikely to be repeated, there are other possibilities closer at hand. Considerable space is contained on six floors in the four corners of the terminal. It is windowless and not suitable for housing or office quarters, but natural light is not essential for either retail areas, communications centers, or performance space. Because New York is as much the seat of communication and information exchange as any part of the nation, it seems reasonable to assume that Grand Central could again assert itself as a gateway.

□ We need a management plan that is far-reaching and comprehensive enough to ensure that the necessary commercial activities are orchestrated into an overall design that reinforces the terminal's basic architectural intent. To achieve any successful and lasting program of operation, maintenance, and improvement, those who conceive and implement this plan should come, not from government or industry, but from the dedicated and determined ranks of a concerned citizens group that can then enlist the best efforts of the private and public sectors in a program it can prove will be to the profit of both. The public cares intensely about the future of the terminal. Leadership is all that is required to ensure its more enlightened use.

□ The Central Park Conservancy funds projects and pays for the Central Park Administrator with private donations. This position is officially recognized by the City of New York, one of many such precedents for a partnership between the public and private sectors. A new partnership would enable the MTA to maintain and operate the terminal as a railroad station in much the same way as Central Park is run by the Parks Department; a private developer would operate retail activities, guaranteeing an annual percentage of the profits to maintain the terminal, and a nonprofit entity would watch over and coordinate the activities of both.

□ The genius of cities is their capacity to renew themselves as technology, social conditions, and economics change. New York is not the city it was nor the one it will be. The same is true of Grand Central Terminal itself. Attempts to celebrate past grandeurs often obscure present realities, but Grand Central's great virtues stem from unabashed faith in the future and the ability to think big. It is an extraordinarily generous and optimistic structure, and any consideration of its future should be no less brave if future generations are to experience its joys as we now know them.

□ We have briefly outlined the types of change that are transforming an astonishing legacy, in an attempt to show that its landmark designation does not ensure its life after survival. At the same time we have considered what actions might best shape the powerful forces now loose in its marbled halls. Unlike nature, the preservation of buildings requires constant maintenance. Although the MTA has cleaned and relit the terminal's interior, and Donald Trump, carrying out his agreement with the city, has cleaned the building's exterior, the viaduct (whose uncertain ownership impedes maintenance efforts) is in need of major reconstruction; the retail spaces are not hallmarks of sophisticated merchandising; the terminal's major access points remain clotted with parked cars; and many of its public areas are unkempt.

□ As the onrush of technology spews out distractions and enticements for the self-centered, the idea of great public spaces in which the public joins together to embrace the common good seems old-fashioned. Nonetheless, without some sense of shared purpose, it will not be possible to hold America's diversity together. Surely our symbols of great undertaking have a value beyond their physical dimension. Grand Central Terminal proves that the forces which shape cities need not be mean and exploitative. It provides not only a measure by which to judge present urban endeavors, but the real means to enhance the future city.

□ It was in New York that Warren and Wetmore realized their best-known and most extensive projects, Grand Central Terminal and a number of hotels adjacent to it. These included the Belmont (1906), the Biltmore (1914), the Commodore (1919), and the Vanderbilt (1912-1913). The firm also designed apartment buildings on Park Avenue, hotels and railroad stations in Canada and the United States, many private residences, the interiors of several ships, and the New York Central Building, constructed in 1929.

Whitney Warren
1864-1943

■ Whitney Warren came from an upper-class family of means and carved a life out of a commitment to professional excellence, the ideals of the Beaux-Arts system of design, and his love for an elegant and refined manner of existence. Born in New York City, Warren attended Columbia College for one year and then went to Paris to study at the Ecole des Beaux-Arts with Daumet and Girault. He remained in France until 1894, and developed a profound appreciation for all things French, particularly for its art and architecture. It was a sympathy that would affect the character of his work throughout his life.

□ Warren's highly successful partnership in New York with Charles Wetmore gave him the opportunity to create some of the great hotels and distinguished office buildings of New York, as well as one of the nation's most important buildings, Grand Central Terminal. Among a great variety of cultural activities both national and international, Warren was founder of the Society of Beaux-Arts Architects in 1894 – in 1911 to become the Beaux-Arts Institute of Design – a group which promoted the Beaux-Arts atelier system of architectural education in America. He was active in the organizing of the annual Beaux-Arts Ball in New York, from its inception in 1913 to the final gala in 1937. Because of his dedication to European political and cultural affairs, he was awarded a number of high honors by the governments of France, Italy, and Belgium. Warren retired from practice in 1931. He died in New York in 1943.

Charles Wetmore
1866-1941

■ Charles Delevan Wetmore was born in Elmira, N.Y. in 1866 and grew up in Jamestown, N.Y. He was graduated from Harvard College and then from Harvard Law School in 1892, but had a strong interest in architecture, demonstrated by the fact that he designed three dormitories at Harvard before joining the law firm of Carter, Ledyard & Milburn. He practiced law there until his fortuitous meeting with Whitney Warren in 1898, from which he gained both a country house and a new profession.

□ Within the partnership, Wetmore had particular responsibility for the Royal Hawaiian Hotel in Honolulu (1927), the Ritz-Carlton in Montreal (1911), the railroad station in Winnipeg (1909), and the Equitable Trust Company building on Madison Avenue in Manhattan (1918).

Reed and Stem

■ The architectural firm of Reed and Stem was formed in St. Paul, Minnesota in the mid-1880s by Charles Reed and Allen Stem. By 1911, when Reed died, the partnership had completed numerous railroad stations for the New York Central, the Great Northern, the Northern Pacific, the Great Western, the Michigan Central, and the Norfolk and Western railroads. The partners' choice of architectural style for a particular station was always appropriate to its location: Their New York Central station at Scarsdale (1904) was fittingly domestic in scale and style, while the one at industrial Troy, N.Y. is a formal Beaux-Arts design.

□ For the design and building of Grand Central, the firm collaborated with Warren and Wetmore under the name of the Associated Architects.

Charles Reed
1858-1911

■ Charles Reed is credited as the chief designer of Reed and Stem's winning competition scheme for Grand Central Terminal. He attended the Massachusetts Institute of Technology, and he served as the executive head of the Associated Architects for the design of Grand Central.

Allen Stem
1856-1931

■ Allen H. Stem was born in Van Wert, Ohio in 1856. His father was a carpenter and a farmer. Stem began practicing architecture in Indianapolis after completing art school there in 1880. He joined in partnership with Charles Reed in St. Paul. Stem designed many projects there, including the Metropolitan Opera House (1890), the Hotel St. Paul (1909), and the St. Paul Athletic Club (1918), as well as buildings in other cities, such as the Denver Auditorium in Colorado (1908). After Reed's death, Stem went into partnership with Alfred Felheimer, who was to become one of the nation's leading architects of railroad stations.

John B. Snook
1815-1901

■ John Snook was the architect of the first major building on the site of Grand Central Terminal, the Grand Central Depot of 1869-1871. In its time, the depot was one of the largest railroad stations in the world. Snook was a highly successful practitioner, and the work of his firm, John B. Snook and Son, provided New York with some of the outstanding cast iron buildings that still impart elegance to lower Manhattan. These include: 10-12 Greene Street (1869); 65 Greene Street (1873); 66-68 Greene Street (1873); 165-171 Grand Street (1849); 287 Broadway (1872); and 341 Broadway (1860).

William J. Wilgus
1865-1949

■ In the nineteenth century, it was the railroad that offered to the creative technical mind the drama and challenge that space travel presents to us now. William Wilgus, born in Buffalo, N.Y. in 1865, was a man of extraordinary creativity, and his energies and intelligence brought him the opportunity to change the history of transportation.

□ Wilgus was graduated from high school in 1883 and studied civil engineering for two years. Starting out as a rodman and then a draughtsman for the Minnesota and Northwestern Railroad, he soon rose to division engineer by 1890. In that capacity, he was responsible for the design and construction of major railroad terminals in Minneapolis and Kansas City, and was in charge of construction and surveying for several other midwestern lines. In 1892, he married May Reed, sister of the architect Charles Reed.

□ From 1893 to 1897, Wilgus was assistant engineer of the Rome, Watertown and Ogdensburg Railroad, part of the New York Central and Hudson River Railroad. In 1897 he became resident engineer, and by 1899 he was chief engineer of the railroad, supervising bridge construction and track improvement of all railroad property at the time of the important changeover from steam to electricity during the early planning for Grand Central Terminal. He can be thought of as the intellectual creator of Grand Central Terminal, and it was he who conceived of the urbanistic possibilities inherent in the use of electrified trains in cities. Wilgus became vice-president of the New York Central in 1903 and remained with the railroad until 1907, when he went into private engineering practice. Active in regional transportation planning, he was involved with such imaginative projects as the tunnel under the Detroit River and a proposal for a railroad tunnel under the Narrows in New York (1921-1922). He retired in 1937.

□ In the First World War Wilgus was a director of transportation for the American Expeditionary Force, and again in 1941 he was an adviser to the War Department. He died in 1949 in Claremont, New Hampshire.

Warren and Wetmore

■ In 1898, Charles Wetmore, a lawyer with an interest in architecture, commissioned the architect Whitney Warren to design a country house for him. Warren was so impressed with his client's penchant for design that he convinced Wetmore to give up law, and that same year the firm of Warren and Wetmore, Architects, was formed in New York City. The firm was successful and distinguished. The partnership's first important commission was the New York Yacht Club (1899). This was followed by major projects for four railroads: the New York Central, the Michigan Central, the Canadian Northern, and the Erie.

Statistics

Outside Dimensions	301′ × 722′6″.
Main Concourse	160′ × 470′; maximum height 150′. This is longer, higher, and wider than the nave of Notre Dame Cathedral in Paris.
Arched Windows	33′ × 60′.
Total Length of Track	32 miles of track laid for terminal complex. First all-electric signal system in the United States.
Cost of Terminal and Land in 1913 Dollars	Approximately $80 million.
Cost of Terminal in 1980 Dollars	Approximately $1.6 billion (more than 10% of the entire budget of New York City for 1980).
Excavation	Required the movement of 400 carloads of rock every year for ten years. 2,800,000 cubic yards of earth and rock excavated.
Highest Passenger Usage	1947: 65 million passengers served, or over 40% of the entire population of the United States at that time.
	1944-1947: an average of 520 trains accommodated per weekday.
Total Complex of Grand Central and Associated Railroad Properties by 1934	Eight hotels: Commodore,** Biltmore,** Roosevelt, Marguery,* Chatham,* Barclay, Park Lane,* Waldorf-Astoria. Eight apartment buildings: 220 Park Avenue,* 277 Park Avenue,* 290 Park Avenue,* 300 Park Avenue,* 320-330 Park Avenue,* 340-350 Park Avenue,* 400 Park Avenue,* 420-430 Park Avenue. Ten office buildings: 466 Lexington Avenue, 420 Lexington Avenue (Graybar Building), Vanderbilt Concourse Building, Grand Central Terminal Building, New York Central Building, Grand Central Palace,* Park-Lexington Building,* 385 Madison Avenue, Postum Building (250 Park Avenue), 379 Madison Avenue.* Also: The Yale Club.

* Demolished
** Dramatically altered

Location	42nd Street and Park Avenue
Dates of Construction	1903-1913
Architects	Reed and Stem Warren and Wetmore
Chief Engineer	William J. Wilgus
Owner	Penn Central Transportation Company
Lessee	Metropolitan Transportation Authority
Structure	Steel frame clad in stone. Terminal complex required approximately 18,600 tons of steel, two times as much used in the New York City subways in 1913, and two-and-a-half times the amount used to build the Eiffel Tower.
Contractor for Excavation and Trackage	O'Rourke Engineering and Construction Company
Building Contractor	John Pierce Company
Exterior	Stony Creek, Connecticut granite and Bedford, Indiana limestone. Roof: ornamental copper. Windows: ornamental steel sash. Heroic sculpture: "Glory of Commerce" (Mercury); "Moral Energy" (Hercules); "Mental Energy" (Minerva). Designed by Jules-Alexis Coutan. Executed by Donnelly and Ricci and by William Bradley and Sons.
Interior	Floors: Tennessee marble. Ornamental trim: Italian Bottocino marble. Ceiling: Plaster vault suspended from steel trusses, showing night sky from October to March with 2,500 stars. Designed by Paul Helleu. Executed by Charles Bassing. Walls: simulated Caen stone. Passage to Graybar Building: mural of Transportation and Construction painted by Edward Trumball, 1931.

Brief Chronology

1869	New York Central and Hudson River Railroad, headed by "Commodore" Cornelius Vanderbilt, begins construction of the first Grand Central. Site popularly ridiculed as "the end of the world."
1871	First Grand Central Depot opens at present site: 164 long-distance and commuting trains accommodated daily. Architect: John Snook. Train shed largest in the world (200' × 600').
1872-1874	Tracks lowered below grade on Fourth Avenue from the depot to 56th Street. Tracks set in tunnel from 56th to 96th streets.
1898	Depot enlarged with three new floors and new facade. Architect: Bradford L. Gilbert.
1899-1903	Conceptualization of a totally electrified Grand Central Terminal, with air rights over railroad land. Principal generator of these ideas: William J. Wilgus.
1900	Depot interior renovated. Architect: Samuel Huckel, Jr.
1902	15 die in accident under Park Avenue as one train rams another in smoke-filled tunnel. New York State passes legislation requiring total electrification by 1908.
1903	Limited architectural competition for design of new terminal. Entries by Daniel H. Burnham; McKim, Mead and White; Samuel Huckel, Jr.; and Reed and Stem. Reed and Stem chosen to design new terminal. Warren and Wetmore selected as associate architects.
1913	Present terminal completed.
1954	80-story tower proposed over baggage-handling area by developer William Zeckendorf. Architect: I. M. Pei for Webb and Knapp.
1958	Skyscraper proposed by developer Erwin Wolfson, and Emery and Richard Roth, architects for present Pan Am Building. Subsequently redesigned by Walter Gropius and Pietro Belluschi.
1960	Scheme proposed to divide waiting room horizontally into four fifteen-foot-tall stories, three for bowling alleys.
1962	Pan Am Building completed (59 stories).
1965	New York City Landmarks Preservation Commission established.
1967	Morris Saady of UGP Properties, Ltd., in an agreement with Penn Central, proposes a new tower over terminal (55 stories); Architect: Marcel Breuer.
1968	Certificate of Acceptability denied by Landmarks Commission.
1969	Penn Central proposes alternate Breuer scheme (59 stories). Certificate of Acceptability denied by Landmarks Commission. Penn Central files a lawsuit against the City in the Supreme Court of the State of New York.
1975	Committee to Save Grand Central Station formed. Justice Irving H. Saypol of the Supreme Court of the State of New York files a decision invalidating the landmark designation for Grand Central. The Appellate Division of the State of New York reverses the lower court decision, upholding the decision of the Landmarks Preservation Commission.
1977	Penn Central appeals the decision to the highest court in the state, the New York Court of Appeals. The City of New York files its brief and the Committee to Save Grand Central files an amicus brief on its own behalf and that of other civic groups. The Court of Appeals unanimously upholds the landmark restrictions. Penn Central prepares to appeal to the U.S. Supreme Court.
1978	On June 26, 1978, in *Penn Central Transportation Company* v. *City of New York,* the Supreme Court upholds the landmark status of Grand Central Terminal. This list was updated and developed from a fact sheet prepared in 1977 by Hugh Hardy on behalf of the Committee to Save Grand Central Station.

Elaine Abelson is a Teaching Fellow at New York University, completing her Ph.D. in American history. She has concentrated her work in nineteenth-century urban and social history.

David Bonderman is a member of the Washington, D.C. law firm of Arnold & Porter. He has represented a variety of preservation groups in recent litigation. On behalf of the National Trust for Historic Preservation and other groups, he filed a brief in the Supreme Court in the *Penn Central* case.

Hugh Hardy is founding partner of the architectural firm of Hardy Holzman Pfeiffer Associates, which designed the Grand Central Terminal: City Within the City exhibition. He was an early member of the Committee to Save Grand Central Station.

Deborah Nevins is an architectural and landscape historian and a curator. She is the coauthor of *Two Hundred Years of American Architectural Drawing* and *The Architect's Eye*.

Milton R. Newman is an architect, lawyer, and past member of the New York Planning Department's Urban Design Group.

Elliot Willensky is an architect, coauthor of the American Institute of Architects' *A.I.A. Guide to New York City*, and a member of New York City's Landmarks Preservation Commission.

Book design by Keith Godard of Works
Design assistant, Jeri Froehlich
Printing by The Georgian Press Inc.
Binding by A. Horowitz & Sons
Typesetting by Southern New England
Typographic Service Inc.

T – Top; M – Middle; B – Bottom; L –Left; R – Right.

Albany Institute of History and Art, McKinney Library: pp. 52T, 57T, 113.
American Telephone & Telegraph: p. 127 BR.
Avery Library, Columbia University: pp. 13TR, 16TL, 18L, 32–33, 35, 36, 37L, 38, 43, 44, 45T, 46–47, 49B, 74–75B, 75T; *The American Architect and Building News*: pp. 12T, 17; *Harper's Weekly*: pp. 15MR, 26B; *The Inland Architect*: p. 26M; *Report of the New York City Improvement Commission to the Honorable George McClellan, 1907*: p. 14; *Scientific American*: pp. 15TLR, 15BL, 15ML, 24B, 25BT, 26T, 34TL, 34B, 72. (Copywork by Otto Nelson.)
Conrail: pp. 37R, 39–42 (NYCRR Track Schematic).
The Cooper-Hewitt Museum, The Smithsonian Institution's National Museum of Design: pp. 27B, 28B.
Davis, Brody & Associates: endpapers.
Collection of Beatrice Greenough: p. 142TR.
Hardy Holzman Pfeiffer Associates: pp. 29, 82LR, 129.
Kalmbach Publishing Company: pp. 45B, 52B, 53, 73B, 111.
Le Corbusier: Oeuvre Complete, Willy Boesiger, editor (Zurich: Ginsberger, *n.d.*): p. 126TR.
The Library of Congress: pp. 21M, 73TM, 110, 119.
Collection of Barbara Millstein: p. 48TB.
Minnesota Historical Society: p. 142BR.
Municipal Archives of the City of New York: pp. 51, 124BR.
Museum of the City of New York, Byron Collection: p. 79B; Print Archives: pp. 16BLR, 19T, 21T, 30, 31TB, 49T, 55, 56B, 60, 61T, 65TB, 78TL, 79TLR, 86TR.
The New-York Historical Society: pp. 12BLR, 15BR, 19B, 20TLR, 20B, 22TB, 27T, 56TB, 58–59, 61MB, 62–63, 66–67, 69TB, 70–71, 76BR, 80BR, 84, 86TR, 109, 114, 117, 122TL, 127BR, 142TL; *Harper's Weekly*: p. 115.
New York Public Library, Local History Collection: pp. 12M, 13TL, 13BL, 23T, 23B, 24T, 28T, 64, 68, 74T, 76TLR, 76BL, 77, 80BL, 81, 90, 92.
New York Streets for People: New Designs for City Spaces (New York: City of New York and Office of Midtown Planning and Development, May 1975): p. 124ML.
New York Times Pictures: p. 142BL.
Collection of Robert A. Olmsted: pp. 16TR, 21BLR.
Cervin Robinson: pp. 50, 80T.
Laura Rosen: pp. 121, 122 (not TL), 123, 124 (not BR, MR, ML), 125, 126 (not ML, MR, TR), 127 (not BR), 135, 136, 138, 139, 141.
Skyviews Survey, Inc.: p. 83.
Speer-Archiv: p. 126MR.
Studio Chevojon (Paris): p. 18R.
Water Street Access and Development (New York: City of New York, Office of Lower Manhattan Development, and Office of the Mayor, 1976): p. 124MR.
John H. White, Jr. *Horsecars, Cable Cars and Omnibuses* (New York: Dover, 1974): p. 86TL.
Collection of Elliot Willensky: pp. 94, 96, 98, 100, 102, 104, 106; Clarence P. Hornung, *The Way It Was* (New York: Schocken Books, 1977): pp. 57B, 86M, 86BR, 88MR, 88BR; Rev. J. F. Richmond, *New York and Its Institutions, 1609–1890* (New York: E.B. Treat, 1872): pp. 86BL, 88TLR, 88ML, 88BL.